Statistics Canada

Housing, Family and Social Statistics Division

A Portrait of Seniors in Canada

Third Edition

Published by authority of the Minister responsible for Statistics Canada

October 1999

Catalogue no. 89-519-XPE

Frequency: Occasional

ISBN 0-660-17769-2

Ottawa

La version française de cette publication est disponible sur demande (n° 89-519-XPF au catalogue).

Note of appreciation

Canada owes the success of its statistical system to a long-standing co-operation involving Statistics Canada, the citizens of Canada, its businesses, governments and other institutions. Accurate and timely statistical information could not be produced without their continued co-operation and goodwill.

Canadian Cataloguing in Publication Data

Lindsay, Colin
A portrait of seniors in Canada

3rd ed.
Issued also in French under title: Un portrait des aînés au Canada.
ISBN 0-660-17769-2
CS89-519-XPE

1. Aged – Canada – Statistics. 2. Aged – Housing – Canada – Statistics.
3. Aged – Health and hygiene – Canada – Statistics. 4. Aged – Canada – Economic conditions – Statistics. 5. Aged women – Canada – Statistics.
I. Statistics Canada. Housing, Family and Social Statistics Division.
II. Title: A portrait of seniors in Canada.

HQ1064.C3 L56 1999 305.26'0971021
C99-988036-5

Symbols

The following standard symbols are used in Statistics Canada publications:

.. figures not available.

... figures not appropriate or not applicable.

- nil or zero.

-- amount too small to be expressed.

p preliminary figures.

r revised figures.

x confidential to meet secrecy requirements of the Statistics Act.

The paper used in this publication meets the minimum requirements of American National Standard for Information Sciences - Permanence of Paper for Printed Library Materials, ANSI Z39.48 - 1984.

Table of Contents

Table of Contents

Acknowledgements

This report was prepared by Colin Lindsay and Marcia Almey of the Target Groups Project of Statistics Canada. The authors gratefully acknowledge the assistance of Monique Hickey, Fiona Mac Donald, Alex Solis, Mario Lisciotto, Colleen Thompson, Shirley Li, Judy Cotterill, Kirstin Wood, Jeanne MacDonald, and Lise Champagne in the preparation and distribution of this report.

The Target Groups Project also acknowledges the generous financial and collaborative support of Health Canada, Veterans Affairs Canada, Human Resources Development Canada, and Canadian Heritage in the development of this report.

Questions or comments pertaining to this report should be addressed to Colin Lindsay, Target Groups Project, Housing, Family and Social Statistics Division, Statistics Canada, 7th Floor, Jean Talon Building, Ottawa, Ontario, K1A 0T6; Telephone: (613) 951-2603; Fax: (613) 951-0387; or e-mail: lindcol@statcan.ca.

Highlights

- Seniors constitute one of the fastest growing population groups in Canada. In 1998, there were an estimated 3.7 million Canadians aged 65 and over, up 57% from 2.4 million in 1981. In contrast, the population in age ranges under age 65 grew by less than 20% in the same period. By 1998, seniors made up 12% of the total population, up from 10% in 1981 and just 5% in 1921.

- The senior population is expected to grow even more rapidly during the next several decades, particularly once people born during the Baby Boom years from 1946 to 1965 begin turning age 65 in the second decade of the new century. Statistics Canada has projected that by 2041, 23% of all Canadians will be aged 65 and over.

- The fastest growth in the number of seniors is occurring among those in older age ranges. In 1998, there were an estimated 380,000 people aged 85 and over in Canada, almost double the number in 1981 (196,000) and close to 20 times more than in 1921, when there were only 21,000 Canadians in this age range.

- The senior population in Canada is predominantly female. In 1998, women represented 57% of Canadians aged 65 and over, whereas they made up just over half (51%) of those aged 55 to 64 and 50% or less of those in age groups under age 55. Women also account for particularly large shares of the older segments of the senior population; that year, women made up 70% of all persons aged 85 and older and 60% of those aged 75 to 84, compared with 54% of people aged 65 to 74.

- Seniors make up a relatively large share of the population in all provinces. In 1998, the seniors' share of provincial populations ranged from 15% in Saskatchewan to 10% in Alberta.

- In 1996, 27% of the population aged 65 and over were immigrants, whereas immigrants made up only 17% of the overall Canadian population. On the other hand, seniors made up relatively small proportions of both the visible minority and Aboriginal identity populations.

- The vast majority of Canadian seniors — 93% in 1996 — live at home in a private household and most live with their family. That year, 57% were living with their husband or wife, 1% were living with their common-law partner and 4% were lone parents. In addition, almost a quarter of a million (240,000) seniors, 7% of the total, lived with members of their extended family.

- While most Canadian seniors live with their family, in 1996, over 900,000 people aged 65 and over, 29% of all seniors, were living on their own.

- Senior women in older age ranges are, by far, the most likely Canadians to live alone. In 1996, well over half (58%) of women aged 85 and over, and almost half (49%) of those aged 75 to 84, lived alone.

Highlights

- For the most part, Canadian seniors look after themselves. Still, in 1996, 84% of all people aged 65 and over received some kind of assistance with household work and other personal chores. Most seniors who get help receive it from family members or friends. In 1997, though, 10% of seniors got support from a home care service.

- While most seniors live in a private household, a substantial number live in an institution. In 1996, just over 250,000 people aged 65 and over, 7% of all seniors in Canada, lived in an institution, with most living in special care homes for the elderly and chronically ill.

- Seniors in older age ranges, especially women, are the most likely to reside in an institution. In 1996, 38% of women aged 85 and over and 24% of men in this age range were in an institution, compared with just 2% of both men and women aged 65 to 74.

- A substantial majority of seniors own their homes. In 1997, 68% of all households headed by someone aged 65 and over owned their home. As well, almost nine out of 10 of these senior homeowners had paid off their mortgage.

- The remaining life expectancy of Canadian seniors has risen substantially over the course of this century. As of 1996, a 65-year-old person had an estimated remaining life expectancy of 18.4 years, roughly a half a year more than in 1991, three years more than in 1971, and five years more than in 1921. As in other age groups, senior women have a longer remaining life expectancy than senior men: 20.2 years for a woman aged 65 in 1996, compared with 16.3 years for her male counterpart.

- Gains in life expectancy among Canadian seniors reflect long-term declines in death rates among people in this age group. Between 1980 and 1996, the age-standardized death rate among people aged 65 and over fell 12%. Death rates, however, are considerably higher among men than among women in this age range.

- Heart disease and cancer account for over half the deaths of Canadian seniors. In 1996, 30% of all deaths of people aged 65 and over were attributed to heart disease and 26% were from cancer. The age-standardized death rate due to heart disease among seniors, though, was 34% lower in 1996 than in 1980, whereas the figure for cancer rose 9% in the same period.

- Much of the increase in the overall cancer death rate among seniors is accounted for by increases in deaths from lung cancer, particularly among senior women. Senior men, however, are still considerably more likely than their female counterparts to die from lung cancer.

- Most seniors living at home describe their general health in positive terms. In 1996-97, 78% said their health was either good (38%), very good (28%), or excellent (12%), while 16% reported their health was fair and only 6% described it as poor.

- While most seniors report their overall health is relatively good, 82% of those living at home in 1996-97 reported they had been diagnosed with at least one chronic health condition, with arthritis and rheumatism the most common chronic health problems. In addition, 28% of these seniors reported some level of restriction in their activities because of a long-term health problem.

- As well, 25% of seniors living at home in 1996-97 had a long-term disability or handicap.

- Seniors are generally less likely than people in younger age groups to suffer injuries serious enough to limit normal activities. In 1996-97, 6% of all people aged 65 and over suffered such an injury, compared with 8% of 55- to 64-year-olds and 10% of those between the ages of 25 and 54.

- Seniors make up a relatively large share of the population that is hospitalized. In 1996-97, there were three times as many hospital separations for every 100,000 people aged 65 and over as there were among people aged 45 to 64. Seniors also tend to stay in hospital for longer periods than younger people.

- The majority of seniors take some form of prescription or over-the-counter medication. In 1996-97, 84% of all people aged 65 and over living at home took some form of medication in the two days prior to the survey. Indeed, 56% had taken two or more medications in this period. Pain relievers were the medication most often taken by seniors.

- Seniors have relatively low levels of formal education. As of 1996, only 8% of all Canadians aged 65 and over had a university degree, while 25% had attended, but had not graduated from high school and 37% had less than a Grade 9 education.

- Partly as a result of their relative lack of formal educational experience, many seniors have difficulty reading. In 1994, over half (53%) of all Canadians aged 66 and over were able to perform only simple reading tasks, such as locating one piece of information in a text.

- Relatively few senior households are connected to the Internet. In 1997, only 4% of households headed by someone aged 65 and over had Internet service, compared with 15% of households with head under age 65. The proportion of senior households with an Internet connection that year, however, was double what it was just a year earlier, when the figure was only 2%.

- While the majority of Canadians seniors are retired, a substantial number are still part of the paid workforce. In 1998, just over 225,000 people aged 65 and over, 6% of the total senior population, had jobs.

- Almost two out of three employed seniors are either self-employed or unpaid family workers. As well, in 1998, 41% of employed seniors only worked part-time. Of those seniors that are employed, a relatively large share work in agriculture. In 1998, seniors represented 10% of the total agricultural workforce in Canada. They also made up 14% of all people employed in religious professions.

Highlights

- While relatively few seniors are still in the paid workforce, many stay active in their communities through participation in formal volunteer activities. In 1997, more than 800,000 Canadians aged 65 and over, 23% of the total senior population, participated in these kinds of activities. At the same time, 58% participated in informal volunteer activities outside their homes.

- Many seniors also contribute to volunteer activities by making financial donations. In 1997, 80% of all seniors made at least one such contribution. That year, seniors donated an average of $328 to charities, more than any other age group.

- The average income of seniors in 1997 was 18% higher than it was in 1981, once the effects of inflation have been accounted for, whereas the figure among people aged 15 to 64 actually declined in the same period. Seniors, however, still have lower incomes, on average, than people in most age groups under age 65.

- The largest share of the income of seniors, 29% in 1997, came from the Old Age Security program, while 21% came from private retirement pensions, 21% came in the form of Canada and Quebec Pension Plan benefits, 12% came from investments other than Registered Retirement Savings Plans, 8% was income from employment, and 5% was income from RRSPs.

- Most of the gains in the overall average incomes of seniors, however, have come from work-related pensions. Between 1981 and 1997, the share of the income of seniors coming from C/QPP doubled from 10% to 21%, while the share from private retirement pensions rose from 12% to 21%.

- Less than one in five seniors in Canada lives in a low-income situation. In 1997, almost two-thirds of a million people aged 65 and over, 19% of all seniors, had incomes below Statistics Canada's Low Income Cut-offs. The proportion of seniors with low incomes, however, has fallen sharply over the past 17 years, dropping from 34% in 1980 to 19% in 1997.

- Among unattached seniors, women are considerably more likely than their male counterparts to have low incomes. In 1997, almost half of these women (49%) lived in a low-income situation.

- Television viewing accounts for the largest share of the free time of older persons. In 1997, people aged 60 and over watched television an average of 4.9 hours per day, almost two hours more per day than the figure for those between the ages of 18 and 59. News and public affairs accounted for the largest share of the television-viewing time of older Canadians, over two hours per day that year.

- Many seniors are physically active on a regular basis. In 1997, half (50%) of all people aged 65 and over engaged in regular physical activity, while 12% occasionally took part in such activity. In fact, seniors are only slightly less likely than people in younger age ranges to be physically active on a regular basis.

- Seniors are generally less likely than people in younger age ranges to be the victims of a crime. In 1997, there were 1.5 senior homicide victims for every 100,000 people aged 65 and over, compared with 2.6 among 15- to 24-year-olds, 2.4 among those aged 25 to 44, and 1.7 among those aged 45 to 64. Seniors, though, are still more likely than younger people to feel unsafe when walking alone in their neighbourhoods after dark.

Introduction

The United Nations has designated 1999 as the International Year of Older Persons. The goals of the year are to enhance understanding, harmony, and mutual support across generations, as well as to increase recognition of the contribution of seniors to their families and communities and to encourage all sectors of society to be responsive to a diverse aging population in a rapidly changing world.

The International Year of Older Persons has special relevance in Canada because seniors make up one of the fastest growing groups in this country. As such, many of the issues associated with an aging population, such as the potential demand on the health care system and the maintenance of income and social support, are of increasing interest in Canada. These questions will become even more critical when the population born during the Baby Boom begins turning 65 early in the next century.

This report includes a comprehensive set of indicators describing the demographic profile of seniors, as well as their family and living arrangements, housing, health, work experience, income, and lifestyle characteristics.

The data in the report are primarily national in scope, although a number of key variables include regional breakdowns. As well, where possible, indicators have been disaggregated by older and younger groups of seniors to show the diversity within the senior population. In addition, most indicators are also compared with those of younger age groups, particularly those of people aged 45 to 54 and 55 to 64 in order to highlight the transitional nature of the aging process.

Much of the information in this report was assembled from published sources; however, a number of series include previously unpublished data from sources such as the 1996 Census of Canada, the National Population Health Survey, the National Survey on Giving, Volunteering and Participating, the Survey of Consumer Finances, and the General Social Survey. Those seeking precise information about data comparability and data quality should consult the source publications directly or contact the Target Groups Project at Statistics Canada.

It should also be noted that for all variables, the latest available information is presented. As a result, some series may include data from several different time periods, as well as from different surveys. In these cases, direct comparisons should be made with caution.

In addition, while efforts have been made to describe the situation of seniors in Canada as comprehensively as possible, this report is not exhaustive, and inevitably, certain data gaps exist.

Population Characteristics

A rapidly growing population

Seniors constitute one of the fastest growing population groups in Canada. In 1998, there were an estimated 3.7 million Canadians aged 65 and over, up 57% from 2.4 million in 1981. In contrast, the population in age ranges under age 65 grew by less than 20% in the same period. (Table 1.1)

As a result of these trends, the share of the overall Canadian population accounted for by seniors has risen in the last several decades. In 1998, seniors made up 12% of the total population, up from 10% in 1981 and 8% in 1971. The current figure is also more than twice that in 1921, when only 5% of people living in Canada were aged 65 and over. (Chart 1.1)

The senior population is expected to grow even more rapidly during the next several decades, particularly once people born during the Baby Boom years from 1946 to 1965 begin turning age 65 early in the second decade of the new century. Statistics Canada has projected[1], for example, that by 2016, 16% of all Canadians will be aged 65 and over, and that by 2041, 23% of the population will be seniors. Indeed, it is projected that there will be almost 6 million seniors in Canada by 2016, and that the figure will climb to close to 10 million by 2041.

More very old seniors

The fastest growth in the number of seniors is occurring among those in older age ranges. In 1998, there were an estimated 380,000 people aged 85 and over in Canada, almost double the number in 1981 (196,000) and close to 20 times more than in 1921, when there were only 21,000 Canadians in this age range. (Table 1.2)

As a result, about one in 10 Canadian seniors is now aged 85 and over, compared with about one in 20 earlier in the century. People aged 85 and over currently represent about 1.3% of the total Canadian population, up from 0.8% in 1981 and just 0.2% in 1921.

The number of people aged 85 and over is expected to increase rapidly in the approaching decades. Statistics Canada has projected that there will be almost 1.6 million Canadians aged 85 and over in 2041, more than four times the figure in 1998. Overall, people aged 85 and over are projected to make up 4% of the total population in 2041, compared with 1% in 1998.

Most people in the 85 and over age range are in their late 80s. Still, in 1996, there were more than 85,000 Canadians aged 90 to 94, almost 21,000 aged 95-99, and over 3,000 aged 100 and over[2].

---

[1] *Projections are based on assumptions of medium population growth.*
[2] *Source: Statistics Canada, 1996 Census of Canada.*

While those aged 85 and over represent the fastest growing segment of the senior population, there has also been considerable growth in the number of seniors under age 85. For example, the number of people aged 75 to 84 has almost doubled in the past two decades, rising from 700,000 in 1981 to 1.2 million in 1998. Currently, about one in three seniors is aged 75 to 84, compared with one in four in the early part of the century.

As with the population aged 85 and over, the number of seniors between the ages of 75 to 84 is expected to rise in the coming decades. Statistics Canada has projected that by 2041 there will be 3.6 million Canadians aged 75 to 84, three times the number in 1998. By 2041, seniors aged 75 to 84 are projected to make up 8% of the total Canadian population, double the current figure (4%).

The population aged 65 to 74 has also grown in recent years, although not as rapidly as that in older age ranges. In 1998, there were 2.1 million Canadians in this age range, up over 40% from 1981. Similarly, the number of 65- to 74-year-olds will continue to grow in coming decades, although, again, not as rapidly as the population in older age categories. The number of people aged 65 to 74 is projected to more than double to just under 4.9 million by 2031, but will begin to decline after that, as people born at the peak of the Baby Boom move into older age ranges. By 2041, the number of 65- to 74-year-olds is projected to have dropped to 4.5 million.

Chart 1.1

Seniors as a percentage of the total population, 1921-1998 and projections to 2041

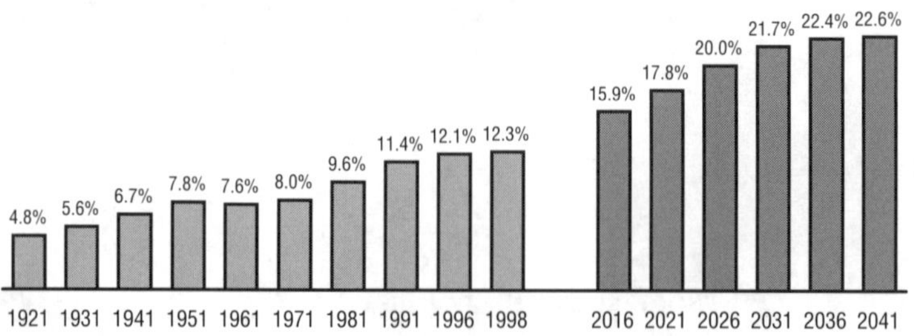

Sources: Statistics Canada, Catalogue nos. 91-213-XPB, 91-520-XPB and 93-310-XPB.

Chart 1.2

Women as a percentage of the population, 1998

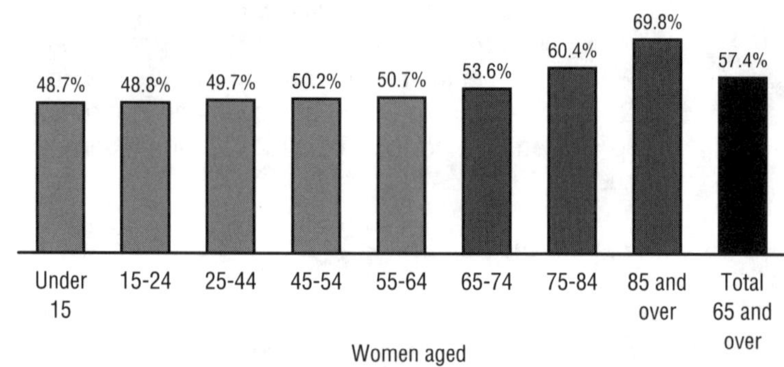

Source: Statistics Canada, Catalogue no. 91-213-XPB.

Senior women in the majority

The senior population in Canada is predominantly female. In 1998, women represented 57% of Canadians aged 65 and over, whereas they made up just over half (51%) of those aged 55 to 64 and 50% or less of those in age groups under age 55. (Chart 1.2)

Women account for particularly large shares of the older segments of the senior population. In 1998, women made up 70% of all persons aged 85 and older and 60% of those aged 75 to 84, compared with 54% of people aged 65 to 74.

The fact that women currently represent a substantial majority of seniors, however, is a relatively recent phenomenon. Indeed, women have only made up more than half of the population aged 65 and over since the 1950s. (Table 1.1)

This shift occurred because the number of senior women grew much faster than the number of senior men during the 1960s and 1970s, as mortality rates among senior women dropped much more rapidly than they did among senior men. As a result, by 1981, the life expectancy[3] of senior women was a full four years longer than that of their male counterparts.

In the past couple of decades, however, the life expectancy of senior men has increased somewhat faster than that of senior women. Consequently, the share of the senior population accounted for by women has fallen slightly in recent years and is expected to dip somewhat further in the next couple of decades. Women, though, are still projected to make up 56% of the senior population throughout the period from 2016 to 2041.

Seniors in the provinces

Seniors attain their largest shares of provincial populations in Saskatchewan and Manitoba, although people aged 65 and over make up a relatively large share of the population in all provinces. In 1998, 15% of all residents of Saskatchewan and 14% in Manitoba were aged 65 and over, while the figure was 13% in British Columbia, Prince Edward Island, Nova Scotia, and New Brunswick; 12% in Ontario and Quebec; 11% in Newfoundland; and 10% in Alberta. (Table 1.3)

While seniors have their largest shares of the provincial populations in Saskatchewan and Manitoba, in terms of absolute numbers, most seniors live in one of the four largest provinces. In 1998, there were almost 1.5 million Ontario residents aged 65 and over, along with just under one million in Quebec, about half a million in British Columbia, and 300,000 in Alberta. Combined, these seniors made up 84% of all seniors in Canada: 38% in Ontario, 24% in Quebec, 14% in British Columbia, and 8% in Alberta. At the same time, there were around 300,000 seniors in Manitoba and Saskatchewan combined and another 300,000 in the Atlantic Provinces; both figures represented about 8% of all seniors in Canada.

Chart 1.3

Net interprovincial migration of seniors, 1997-98

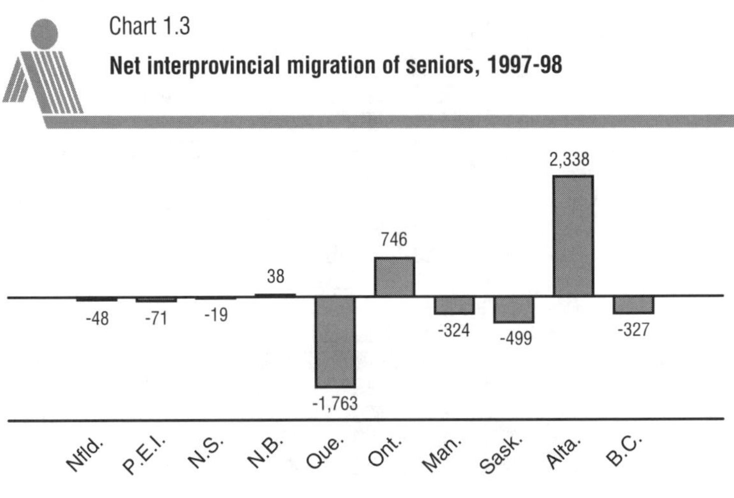

Source: Statistics Canada, Catalogue no. 91-213-XPB.

Interestingly, while seniors make up a relatively small proportion of the population in Alberta, the largest net flow of senior interprovincial migrants is currently into Alberta. In 1997-98, over 2,300 more people aged 65 and over moved into Alberta than moved out. There was also a net in-flow of around 750 seniors into Ontario that year, while there were net out-flows of almost 1,800 seniors out of Quebec, 500 out of Saskatchewan, more than 300 out of British Columbia, and 100 out of the Atlantic Provinces. (Chart 1.3)

The provincial distribution of the population in older age ranges is similar to that for the overall senior population. For example, 81% of all people aged 85 and over lived in one of the four largest provinces in 1998. People in this age range, though, attained the largest share of their respective provincial populations in Saskatchewan (2.0%) and Manitoba (1.7%), while they accounted for the smallest share in Alberta (1.0%). (Table 1.4)

[3] *See the Health Chapter for more detail on trends in life expectancy.*

Women make up a substantial majority of seniors in all provinces. In 1998, the share of the senior population accounted for by women ranged from 59% in Quebec and Nova Scotia to 56% in Newfoundland, Saskatchewan, Alberta, and British Columbia. (Table 1.3)

As at the national level, the share of the senior population accounted for by women rises with age in all provinces. In 1998, women's share of the population aged 85 and over ranged from 73% in Quebec to 65% in Saskatchewan. (Table 1.5)

Urban/rural distribution of seniors

As with the overall population, the large majority of seniors live in an urban area. In 1996, 76% of people aged 65 and over, slightly below the figure for those between the ages of 15 and 64 (79%), lived in an area classified as urban. In contrast, seniors were more likely than younger adults to live in an area classified as rural: 24% versus 21% that year. (Table 1.6)

Within the urban population, seniors are about as likely as their younger counterparts to reside in areas other than a census metropolitan area (CMA)[4], while they are less likely to live in a CMA. In 1996, 17% of seniors, and 16% of people between the ages of 15 and 64, lived in a non-CMA urban area, whereas 59% of seniors, compared with 63% of the adult population under age 65, lived in a CMA.

There is also considerable variation in the share of the population accounted for by seniors in different urban areas across the country. For example, 18% of all residents in Victoria in 1998 were aged 65 and over, while the figure was 16% in St. Catharines-Niagara and 14% in Winnipeg, Hamilton, and Trois-Rivières. In contrast, seniors made up only 10% of people in Edmonton and Halifax and just 9% of those in Calgary and Oshawa. (Chart 1.4)

Seniors also make up a relatively large share of the population in each of three largest CMAs. In 1998, 12% of residents of both Vancouver and Montréal and 11% of those in Toronto were aged 65 and over. That year, 31% of all seniors in Canada lived in one of these three urban areas.

Senior migrants

Seniors are generally less likely than people in younger age groups to make a residential move. In 1996, 176,500 people aged 65 and over, 5% of the total, made a residential move of some kind within the previous year. In contrast, 20% of those aged 25 to 44 and 8% of 45- to 64-year-olds changed residences that year. (Table 1.7)

Chart 1.4

Seniors as a percentage of the population in census metropolitan areas, 1998

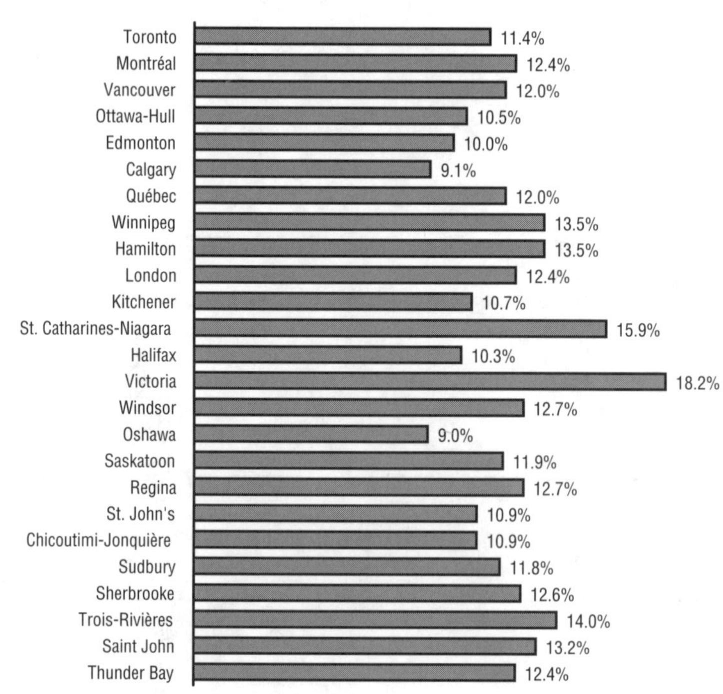

Source: Statistics Canada, Catalogue no. 91-213-XPB.

[4] *A census metropolitan area is an urban area with a population of 100,000 or more.*

Chart 1.5

Immigrants as a percentage of the population living in Canada in 1996

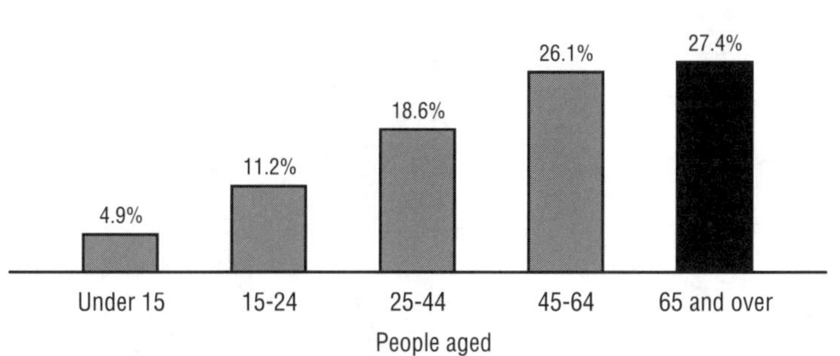

Source: Statistics Canada, 1996 Census of Canada.

Chart 1.6

Period of immigration of immigrants living in Canada in 1996

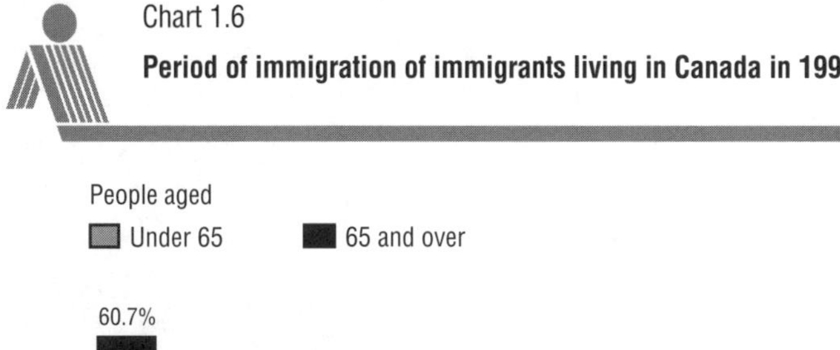

Source: Statistics Canada, 1996 Census of Canada.

As well, most seniors who do move remain within their communities; indeed, more than half of those that moved in 1996 only changed residences within their community. At the same time, one in three senior movers moved from one community to another within the same province, while smaller percentages either moved from one province to another or came from outside Canada.

Senior immigrants

A relatively large proportion of seniors living in Canada are immigrants[5]. In 1996, 27% of the population aged 65 and over were immigrants, whereas immigrants made up only 17% of the overall Canadian population. Indeed, immigrants make up a larger segment of the senior population than they do in any other age category. (Chart 1.5)

Most immigrant seniors currently living in Canada have been in the country for a relatively long period. Of senior immigrants living in Canada in 1996, 61% arrived in the country before 1961, while 14% came in the 1960s and 11% immigrated between 1971 and 1980. In contrast, only 15% have arrived since 1981. (Chart 1.6)

In fact, seniors represent a small share of immigrants currently arriving in Canada each year. In 1997, just under 6,000 people aged 65 and over, only 3% of all those who arrived in Canada that year, immigrated to Canada. (Table 1.8)

As well, almost all senior immigrants currently arriving in Canada are family-class immigrants. Of immigrants aged 65 and over who arrived in Canada in 1997, 90% were family-class immigrants, while 6% were refugees and 4% were economic-class immigrants.

Almost all immigrant seniors have become Canadian citizens. Indeed, 88% of all immigrants aged 65 and over living in Canada in 1996 had taken out Canadian citizenship[2].

Most immigrant seniors are from Europe. As of 1996, 71% of all senior immigrants living in Canada were born in Europe: 38% were from either the United Kingdom or other Western European nation and 34% were from either Eastern or Southern Europe. At the same, 16% were from Asia and 6% were born in the United States, while smaller shares were from other regions. This distribution contrasts sharply with that of younger immigrants, far more of whom come from countries in Asia, Africa, and the Caribbean and Central and South America. (Table 1.9)

[5] *The immigrant population refers to those who have landed-immigrant status, whether or not they are Canadian citizens. It is important to note that children born in Canada to immigrant parents are not included in the immigrant population, but are included in the Canadian-born population.*

Seniors in Canada in an international context

While the Canadian population is aging rapidly, the share of the total Canadian population accounted for by seniors is currently smaller than that in most other developed countries. In 1996, 12% of all people in Canada were aged 65 and over, compared with 13% in the United States and the Netherlands; 15% in Germany, France, Switzerland, and Japan; 16% in the United Kingdom; and 17% in Sweden and Italy. (Table 1.10)

This situation is likely to change within the next several decades, however, because the age cohorts that will begin turning 65 early in the next century are larger in Canada than they are in most of these other countries. For example, 30% of the Canadian population was aged 35 to 54 in 1996, whereas the figure ranged from 29% in Japan, the United States, Switzerland, and the Netherlands to 26% in the United Kingdom, France, and Italy.

Indeed, while seniors currently make up a smaller share of the Canadian population (12%) than that in the United States (13%), people aged 65 and over are projected to make up 18% of the Canadian population in 2021, whereas they are expected to represent only 16% of Americans in 2020[1].

[1] *Source: United States Bureau of the Census, Current Population Reports.*

Language characteristics of seniors

Almost all seniors can speak one or both of Canada's official languages. In 1996, though, 4% of seniors, as opposed to only 1% of those between the ages of 15 and 64, could not speak either English or French. (Table 1.11)

As well, among seniors, women are somewhat more likely than men to be unable to speak either English or French. In 1996, 5.2% of women aged 65 and over, versus 3.5% of their male counterparts, were unable to converse in either official language.

Seniors are also more likely than younger people to speak a language other than one of the official languages in their homes. In 1996, 11% of people aged 65 and over, versus 9% of those between the ages of 15 and 64, spoke only a language other than English or French in their homes. Another 1% of seniors, about the same figure as for those aged 15 to 64, spoke both a non-official language and at least one official language in their home. (Table 1.12)

As with the rest of the population, though, the vast majority of seniors can speak one of the official languages; similarly, most speak either English or French in their homes. In 1996, 69% of all people aged 65 and over could speak English only, 14% could speak French only, and 12% were bilingual. That year, 88% of all seniors spoke one of the official languages in their homes.

Chart 1.7

Religious affiliation, 1996

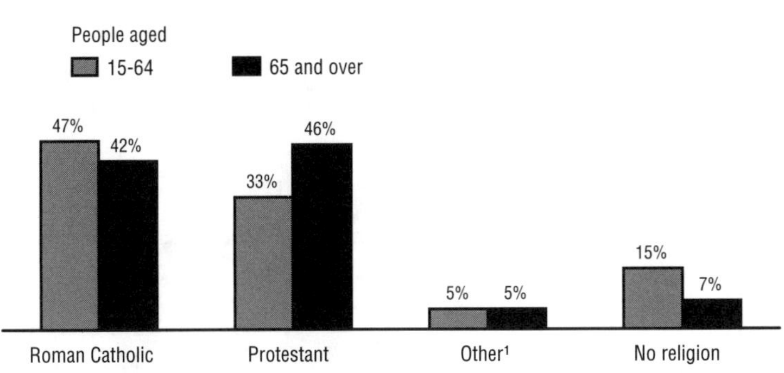

[1] *Includes Jewish, Eastern Orthodox, and other Eastern or Asian religions.*
Source: Statistics Canada, General Social Survey, 1996.

Chart 1.8

Percentage of the population in the visible minority population, 1996

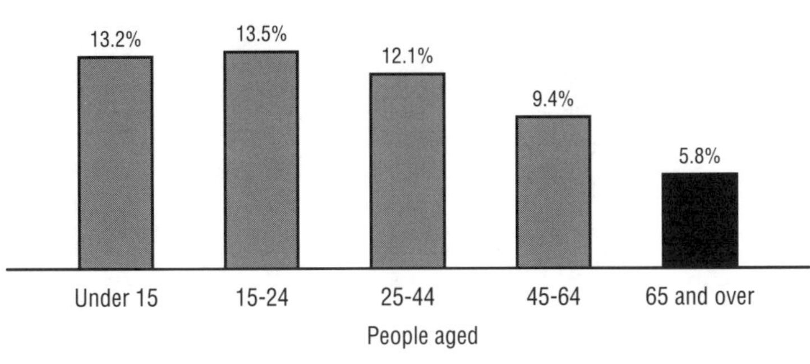

Source: Statistics Canada, 1996 Census of Canada.

Religious affiliation of seniors

The large majority of seniors report some kind of religious affiliation; indeed, seniors are more likely than younger adults to have some religious affiliation. In 1996, 93% of seniors, versus 85% of those between the ages of 15 and 64, reported they were affiliated with some religious group. In contrast, only 7% of seniors, compared with 15% of non-seniors, reported no religious affiliation. (Chart 1.7)

Most seniors are affiliated with either one of the Protestant denominations or the Roman Catholic Church. In 1996, 46% of seniors were affiliated with a Protestant denomination and 42% were Roman Catholic, while just 5% were either Jewish or affiliated with Eastern Orthodox or other Eastern or Asian religions. As well, seniors were considerably more likely than those between the ages of 15 and 64 to be affiliated with a Protestant denomination, while they were less likely to be Roman Catholic.

Few visible minorities

A relatively small proportion of seniors are part of the visible minority population. In 1996, 191,000 people aged 65 and over identified themselves as being members of a visible minority; this represented 6% of the total senior population that year. In contrast, 9% of those aged 45 to 64, 12% of 25- to 44-year-olds, and around 13% of those under age 25 were part of the visible minority population. (Chart 1.8)

The largest number of visible minority seniors are either Chinese, South Asian, or Black. Indeed, people in these three groups made up 72% of all visible minority seniors in 1996: 40% were of Chinese descent, 19% were South Asian, and 13% were Black. (Table 1.13)

The Japanese sub-group, however, is the oldest visible minority group. In 1996, 12% of all those in the Japanese visible minority population, about the same figure as for Canada overall, were aged 65 and over. At the same, 9% of the Chinese group were seniors, whereas only 3% of the Latin American group and 4% of both Blacks and Southeast Asians were aged 65 and over.

Aboriginal seniors

Seniors currently make up a relatively small proportion of the Aboriginal population in Canada. In 1996, just 4% of people who reported they were North American Indian, Métis, or Inuit were aged 65 and over, compared with 12% of the general population. (Chart 1.9)

As with the overall senior population, however, the Aboriginal population aged 65 and over is expected to grow rapidly in the next several decades. The Royal Commission on Aboriginal Peoples estimated that the number of Aboriginal seniors will almost triple between 1996 and 2016, such that by 2016, 7% of all Aboriginal persons will be aged 65 and over[6].

Chart 1.9

Seniors as a percentage of the Aboriginal identity population, 1996

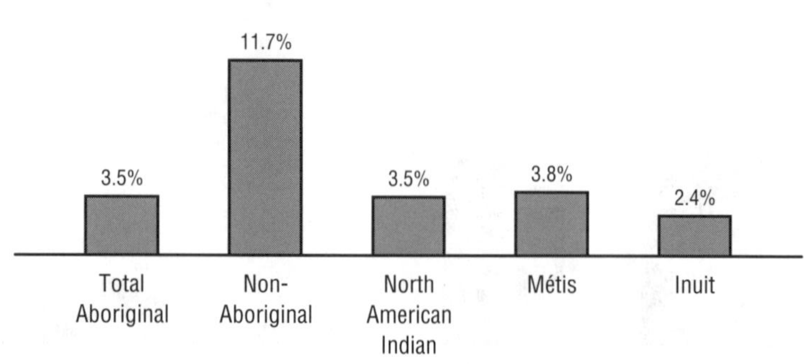

Source: Statistics Canada, 1996 Census of Canada.

Seniors make up a larger share of the North American Indian and Métis populations than they do among the Inuit. In 1996, 4% of those who were either North American Indian or Métis were aged 65 and over, versus only 2% of those who reported they were Inuit.

Among Registered North American Indians, seniors are somewhat more likely to live on reserves than their younger counterparts. In 1996, 67% of Registered North American Indians aged 65 and over lived on reserves, compared with 59% of those under age 65[2].

In addition, seniors are the most likely Aboriginal group to know and use an Aboriginal language. In 1996, 54% of Aboriginal seniors knew how to speak an Aboriginal language, almost twice the figure for Aboriginal people under age 65. Similarly, 35% of Aboriginal people aged 65 and over spoke an Aboriginal language at home, compared with 14% of their counterparts under age 65[2].

Senior veterans

A substantial share of senior men in Canada are veterans of foreign wars. In 1995, 38% of all men aged 65 and over had served in the military during wartime. At the same time, 3% of senior women were also veterans[7].

The largest number of senior veterans fought in the Second World War. In 1995, 36% of men aged 65 and over and 3% of women were Second World War veterans. On the other hand, there are very few surviving veterans of the First World War.

[6] *Projections of the Population with Aboriginal Identity in Canada, 1996-2016, by M.J. Norris, D. Kerr, and F. Nault; Prepared for the Royal Commission on Aboriginal Peoples, May, 1995.*

[7] *Source: Statistics Canada, General Social Survey, 1995.*

Table 1.1

Population aged 65 and over, 1921-1998 and projections to 2041

	People aged 65 and over			People aged 65 and over as a % of total population	Women as a % of population aged 65 and over
	Men	Women	Total		
		000s			
1921	215.0	205.3	420.2	4.8	48.8
1931	294.6	281.5	576.1	5.6	48.9
1941	390.9	376.9	767.8	6.7	49.1
1951	551.3	535.0	1,086.3	7.8	49.2
1961	674.1	717.0	1,391.1	7.6	51.5
1971	790.3	972.0	1,762.3	8.0	55.2
1981	1,017.2	1,360.1	2,377.3	9.6	57.2
1986	1,147.6	1,589.3	2,737.0	10.4	58.1
1991	1,349.8	1,867.4	3,217.2	11.4	58.0
1996	1,515.3	2,066.7	3,582.0	12.1	57.7
1998	1,588.5	2,147.2	3,735.7	12.3	57.4
Projections[1]					
2016	2,591.2	3,302.9	5,894.3	15.9	56.0
2021	3,050.7	3,840.6	6,891.1	17.8	55.7
2026	3,558.1	4,438.8	7,996.9	20.0	55.5
2031	3,976.5	4,960.1	8,936.5	21.7	55.5
2036	4,166.6	5,261.0	9,427.6	22.4	55.8
2041	4,244.8	5,424.6	9,669.6	22.6	56.1

1 *Projections based on assumptions of medium population growth.*

Sources: Statistics Canada, Catalogue nos. 95-537-XPB and 93-310-XPB; and Demography Division.

Table 1.2

Population in age groups over age 65, 1921-1998 and projections to 2041

	Seniors aged					
	65-74		75-84		85 and over	
	000s	As a % of total population	000s	As a % of total population	000s	As a % of total population
1921	290.2	3.3	109.3	1.2	20.8	0.2
1931	402.9	3.9	147.9	1.4	25.3	0.2
1941	524.8	4.6	207.2	1.8	35.8	0.3
1951	748.6	5.3	285.2	2.0	52.5	0.4
1961	889.3	4.9	421.1	2.3	80.8	0.4
1971	1,088.4	5.0	534.7	2.4	139.2	0.6
1981	1,487.0	6.0	694.6	2.8	195.6	0.8
1986	1,673.2	6.4	832.0	3.2	231.8	0.9
1991	1,922.6	6.9	1,006.4	3.6	288.1	1.0
1996	2,090.3	7.0	1,147.0	3.9	344.7	1.2
1998	2,124.7	7.0	1,230.7	4.1	380.3	1.3
Projections[1]						
2016	3,392.2	9.1	1,703.9	4.6	798.2	2.2
2021	4,016.4	10.4	2,015.3	5.2	859.4	2.2
2026	4,528.1	11.3	2,539.5	6.3	929.3	2.3
2031	4,859.3	11.8	2,985.8	7.2	1,091.4	2.6
2036	4,713.0	11.2	3,364.5	8.0	1,350.1	3.2
2041	4,502.9	10.5	3,589.0	8.4	1,577.7	3.7

1 Projections are based on assumptions of medium population growth.
Sources: Statistics Canada, Catalogue nos. 95-537-XPB and 93-310-XPB; and Demography Division.

Table 1.3

Population aged 65 and over, by province, 1998

	000s	As a % of total provincial population	As a % of all people aged 65 and over in Canada	Women as a % of provincial population aged 65 and over
Newfoundland	62.0	11.4	1.7	55.5
Prince Edward Island	17.7	13.0	0.4	58.3
Nova Scotia	123.3	13.2	3.3	58.6
New Brunswick	97.1	12.9	2.6	57.8
Quebec	912.3	12.4	24.4	59.0
Ontario	1,417.9	12.4	38.0	57.4
Manitoba	154.8	13.6	4.1	57.9
Saskatchewan	149.2	14.6	4.0	56.4
Alberta	288.4	9.9	7.7	55.9
British Columbia	509.2	12.7	13.6	56.0
Canada	3,735.7	12.3	100.0	57.4

Source: Statistics Canada, Demography Division.

Table 1.4

Population in age groups over age 65, by province, 1998

	People aged					
	65-74		75-84		85 and over	
	000s	As a % total provincial population	000s	As a % of total provincial population	000s	As a % of total provincial population
Newfoundland	34.9	6.4	21.1	3.9	6.0	1.1
Prince Edward Island	9.3	6.8	6.1	4.4	2.2	1.6
Nova Scotia	65.6	7.0	43.4	4.7	14.2	1.5
New Brunswick	52.6	7.0	33.5	4.4	11.0	1.4
Quebec	537.4	7.3	288.8	3.9	86.1	1.2
Ontario	818.0	7.2	460.4	4.0	139.6	1.2
Manitoba	80.4	7.1	55.1	4.8	19.2	1.7
Saskatchewan	75.4	7.4	53.6	5.2	20.1	2.0
Alberta	165.6	5.7	93.8	3.2	29.1	1.0
British Columbia	282.7	7.1	173.8	4.3	52.6	1.3
Canada	2,124.7	7.0	1,230.7	4.1	380.3	1.3

Source: Statistics Canada, Demography Division.

Table 1.5

Women as a percentage of the population in age groups over age 65, by province, 1998

	Women aged		
	65-74	75-84	85 and over
		%	
Newfoundland	52.1	57.9	67.1
Prince Edward Island	52.7	62.4	69.7
Nova Scotia	54.3	61.0	70.9
New Brunswick	53.9	59.9	70.0
Quebec	54.9	62.4	72.6
Ontario	53.6	60.2	70.4
Manitoba	53.7	60.4	68.7
Saskatchewan	52.4	58.6	65.4
Alberta	52.0	59.0	68.0
British Columbia	52.2	58.9	67.1
Canada	53.6	60.4	69.8

Source: Statistics Canada, Demography Division.

Table 1.6

Urban/rural distribution of the population, 1996

	Census metropolitan area	Other urban area	Total urban	Rural	Total
			%		
People aged:					
Under 15					
Males	60.0	16.1	76.0	24.0	100.0
Females	60.0	16.1	76.1	23.9	100.0
Total	60.0	16.1	76.1	24.0	100.0
15-64					
Men	62.7	15.4	78.2	21.8	100.0
Women	63.6	15.7	79.3	20.7	100.0
Total	63.2	15.6	78.7	21.3	100.0
65 and over					
Men	57.0	16.8	73.9	26.2	100.0
Women	60.3	17.0	77.3	22.7	100.0
Total	58.9	17.0	75.8	24.2	100.0

Source: Statistics Canada, 1996 Census of Canada.

Table 1.7

Mobility status[1], 1996

	People aged		
	25-44	45-64	65 and over
		%	
Non-migrant movers	11.9	4.7	3.0
Intraprovincial migrants	5.9	2.6	1.8
Interprovincial migrants	1.4	0.5	0.3
External migrants	1.0	0.4	0.3
Total movers	20.1	8.4	5.4
Total movers (000s)	1,876.2	516.6	176.5

[1] *Refers to the percentage of the 1996 population living in a different residence than in 1995.*
Source: Statistics Canada, 1996 Census of Canada.

Table 1.8

Immigrants arriving in Canada in 1997, by class

	Immigrants aged	
	Under 65	65 and over
	%	
Family	26.0	89.8
Economic	59.6	3.9
Refugees	11.3	5.6
Other	2.9	0.6
Total	100.0	100.0
Total immigrants	210,164	5,885
% of all immigrants	97.3	2.7

Source: Citizenship and Immigration Canada.

Table 1.9

Immigrants living in Canada in 1996, by region of birth

	Immigrants aged				
	Under 65		65 and over		
	000s	As a % of immigrants under age 65	000s	As a % of immigrants aged 65 and over	Immigrants aged 65 and over as a % of all immigrants
Europe:					
United Kingdom	456.2	11.2	199.3	22.2	30.4
Northern/Western Europe	375.3	9.2	139.0	15.4	27.0
Eastern Europe	290.1	7.1	157.8	17.5	35.2
Southern Europe	567.4	14.0	146.9	16.3	20.6
Total Europe	1,689.1	41.4	643.0	71.4	27.6
United States	190.2	4.7	54.5	6.1	22.3
Central/South America	258.6	6.4	15.2	1.7	5.6
Caribbean	256.8	6.3	22.6	2.5	8.1
Africa	213.1	5.2	16.2	1.8	7.1
Asia:					
West/Central Asia and Middle East	197.0	4.8	13.9	1.6	6.6
Eastern Asia	518.3	12.7	71.1	7.9	12.1
Southeast Asia	382.1	9.4	26.9	3.0	6.6
Southern Asia	322.6	7.9	30.9	3.4	8.7
Total Asia	1,420.0	34.9	142.8	15.9	9.1
Oceania and Other	43.6	1.1	5.5	0.6	11.2
Total	4,071.3	100.0	899.8	100.0	18.1

Source: Statistics Canada, 1996 Census of Canada.

Table 1.10

Percentage of the population in selected age groups in Canada and other countries

	People aged		
	35-54	55-64	65 and over
		%	
Canada (1996)	29.6	8.6	12.1
United States (1996)	28.6	8.1	12.8
Japan (1995)	29.0	12.3	14.5
Australia (1995)	27.5	8.3	11.9
Germany (1995)	27.2	12.6	15.4
Sweden (1995)	27.5	9.7	17.4
Switzerland (1995)	29.1	10.2	15.2
Netherlands (1995)	28.8	9.4	13.2
Italy (1995)	26.4	12.0	16.6
France (1993)	26.0	10.2	14.5
United Kingdom (1995)	26.2	9.9	15.7

Sources: Statistics Canada, Demography Division; and United Nations, 1996 Demographic Yearbook.

Table 1.11

Knowledge of official languages, 1996

	People aged					
	15-64			65 and over		
	Men	Women	Total	Men	Women	Total
			%			
English only	66.9	65.2	66.1	69.6	67.7	68.5
French only	11.9	13.8	12.9	12.2	15.8	14.2
Both English and French	20.3	19.5	19.9	14.7	11.3	12.8
Neither English nor French	0.9	1.4	1.1	3.5	5.2	4.4
Total	100.0	100.0	100.0	100.0	100.0	100.0
Total population (000s)	9,605.1	9,744.1	19,349.2	1,417.4	1,862.4	3,279.8

Source: Statistics Canada, 1996 Census of Canada.

Table 1.12

Home language, 1996

	People aged					
	15-64			65 and over		
	Men	Women	Total	Men	Women	Total
			%			
Official language only	89.5	89.2	89.3	87.1	88.0	87.6
Non-official language only	8.9	9.2	9.0	11.4	10.8	11.1
Official language and non-official language	1.6	1.7	1.6	1.4	1.2	1.3
Total	100.0	100.0	100.0	100.0	100.0	100.0
Total population (000s)	9,605.1	9,744.1	19,349.2	1,417.4	1,862.4	3,279.8

Source: Statistics Canada, 1996 Census of Canada.

Table 1.13

Visible minority seniors, by sub-group, 1996

	Senior visible minority population			
	Total	As a % of all visible minority seniors	As a % of all seniors in Canada	As a % of all persons in visible minority group
		%		
Visible minority sub-group				
Chinese	75,670	39.6	2.3	8.8
South Asian	36,930	19.3	1.1	5.5
Black	24,580	12.9	0.7	4.3
Filipino	13,745	7.2	0.4	5.9
Arab/West Asian	11,815	6.2	0.4	4.8
Japanese	8,245	4.3	0.3	12.1
Southeast Asian	6,680	3.4	0.2	3.8
Latin American	5,170	2.7	0.2	2.9
Korean	3,105	1.6	0.1	4.8
Other	5,130	2.7	0.2	3.9
Total	191,070	100.0	5.8	6.0

Source: Statistics Canada, 1996 Census of Canada.

Living Arrangements and Family Status

Most seniors live in a private household

The vast majority of Canadian seniors live at home in a private household. In fact, in 1996, this was the case for 93% of all people aged 65 and over. The proportion of seniors living at home, though, is less than the figure for the population between the ages of 15 and 64, over 99% of whom lived in a private household that year. (Chart 2.1)

The proportion of seniors living in a private household also declines considerably with age. In 1996, only 66% of all seniors aged 85 and over were living at home, compared with 91% of those aged 75 to 84 and 98% of those aged 65 to 74.

As well, senior men are somewhat more likely than senior women to live in a private household. In 1996, 95% of men aged 65 and over lived at home, versus 91% of their female counterparts. (Chart 2.2)

There is a particularly wide gap between the proportion of senior men and women in older age ranges living at home. In 1996, only 62% of women aged 85 and over resided in a private household, compared with 76% of their male counterparts. In contrast, the share of women aged 75 to 84 living at home (90%) was just slightly below the figure for men in this age range (93%), while there was almost no difference in this figure among those aged 65 to 74; that year, 98% of both women and men in this age group lived at home.

Most seniors live with family

The large majority of seniors living in a private household live with their family, either as a family head or spouse, or with their extended family, such as the family of a daughter or son. In 1996, 69% of all people aged 65 and over lived with family members. That year, 57% were living with their husband or wife, while a small percentage (1%) were living with their common-law partner and 4% were lone parents. (Table 2.1)

Chart 2.1

Percentage of the population living in a private household, 1996

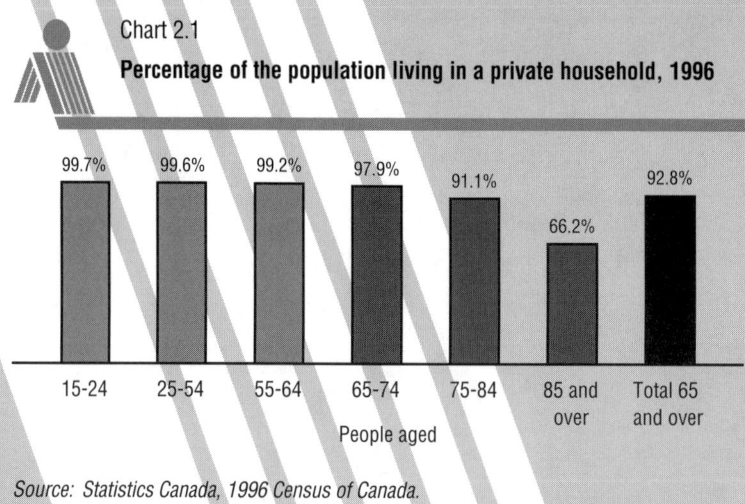

Source: Statistics Canada, 1996 Census of Canada.

Chart 2.2

Percentage of seniors living in a private household, 1996

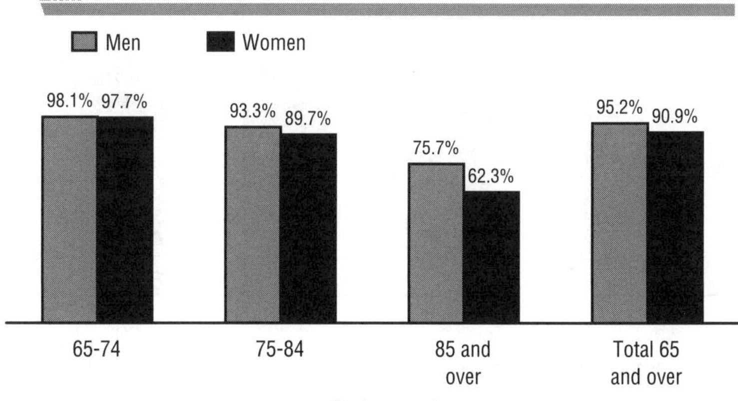

Source: Statistics Canada, 1996 Census of Canada.

Chart 2.3

Percentage of seniors living in an extended family, 1971-1996

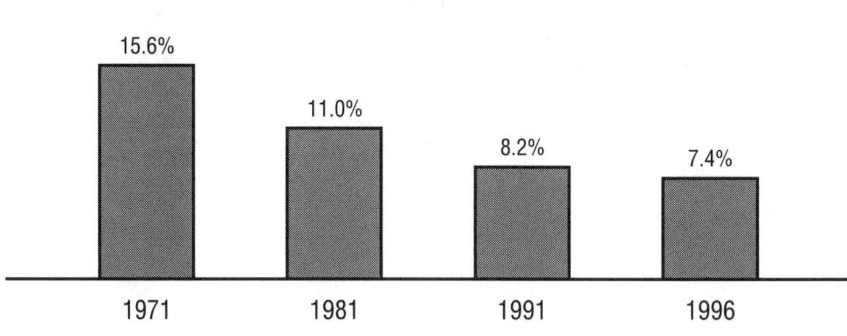

Source: Statistics Canada, Censuses of Canada.

In addition, almost a quarter of a million (240,000) seniors, 7% of the total population aged 65 and over, lived with members of their extended family in 1996. The proportion of seniors who live with their extended family, though, is currently only about half what it was in 1971, when the figure was 16%. (Chart 2.3)

Seniors living alone

While most Canadian seniors live with their family, a substantial number live alone. In 1996, over 900,000 people aged 65 and over, 29% of all seniors, were living on their own. This compared with just 9% of people between the ages of 15 and 64. That year, seniors made up 36% of all people living alone, whereas they represented only 12% of the total population. (Table 2.1)

As well, the proportion of seniors living alone is rising. In 1996, 29% of seniors lived by themselves, up from 27% in 1981 and 20% in 1971. (Chart 2.4)

Differences in family status by age and gender

There are also considerable differences in the family status of Canadian seniors depending on their age and sex. Senior women, for example, especially those in older age ranges, are far less likely than their male counterparts to be living with family members, while they are far more likely to be living alone. In 1996, only 40% of women aged 85 and over and 49% of those aged 75 to 84 lived with members of their family. These figures were both around 30 percentage points below those for men in the same age range. Women aged 65 to 74 were also less likely than their male counterparts to be living with members of their family, although this difference was only about half that for women in older ranges: 69% versus 84%. (Table 2.2)

Relatively few senior women in older age ranges currently live with members of their family, in large part because the percentage of senior women living with their spouse declines sharply with age. In 1996, just 11% of women aged 85 and over, and only 30% of those aged 75 to 84, were living with their spouse, compared with 54% of women aged 65 to 74.

In fact, most senior women in older age ranges are widowed. In 1996, almost 80% of women aged 85 and over were widowed, as were 58% of those aged

75 to 84, whereas this was the case for only 32% of women aged 65 to 74. (Table 2.3)

The proportion of senior men living with their spouse also decreases with age, although the majority of senior men in all age ranges live with their spouse; as well, at all ages, senior men are far more likely than their female counterparts to be living with their spouse. In 1996, 77% of men aged 65 to 74 lived with their spouse, as did 72% of those aged 75 to 84 and 55% of those aged 85 and over. (Table 2.2)

Chart 2.4

Percentage of seniors living alone, 1971-1996

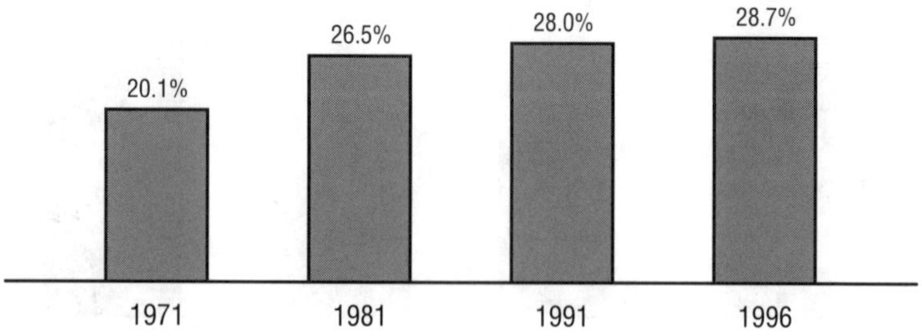

1971	1981	1991	1996
20.1%	26.5%	28.0%	28.7%

Source: Statistics Canada, Censuses of Canada.

The differences in the marital status of senior men and women also partly reflect the fact that senior men are much more likely than senior women to have remarried. In 1995, 9% of men aged 65 and over, versus 5% of women in this age range, had been married more than once. Senior men in older age ranges are even more likely than their female counterparts to have remarried. Among those aged 75 to 84, for example, 13% of men, versus just 3% of women, had been married more than once. Similarly, among those aged 85 and over, 8% of men, but only 1% of women, had remarried[1].

More senior women live with extended family or live alone

While relatively few senior women live with their spouse, a comparatively large number live with members of their extended family. In 1996, 10% of all women aged 65 and over lived with their extended family, compared with just 3% of men in this age range. (Table 2.1)

Senior women in older age ranges are the most likely to live with their extended family. In 1996, 22% of women aged 85 and over lived with members of their extended family, compared with 12% of those aged 75 to 84 and 8% of women aged 65 to 74. (Table 2.2)

Senior women are also far more likely than senior men to live alone. In 1996, 38% of all women aged 65 and over lived on their own, compared with 16% of men in this age range. (Table 2.1)

Again, senior women in older age ranges are, by far, the most likely to live alone. In 1996, well over half (58%) of women aged 85 and over, and almost half (49%) of those aged 75 to 84, lived alone. This compared with around 30% or less of both women aged 65 to 74 and senior men of all ages. (Table 2.2)

Family status of seniors across the country

There is considerable variation in the family status of seniors across the country, although the majority of seniors in all provinces live with members of their family. In 1996, the proportion of seniors living with members of their family

[1] *Source: Statistics Canada, 1995 General Social Survey.*

ranged from 77% in Newfoundland to 65% in each of Saskatchewan and Manitoba. (Table 2.4)

The relatively low proportions of seniors in Saskatchewan and Manitoba living with their family is a reflection, in part, of the fact that few seniors in these two provinces live with members of their extended family. In 1996, just 4% of people aged 65 and over in Saskatchewan, and 5% of those in Manitoba, lived with members of their extended family, while in the other provinces the figure ranged from 6% in Alberta to 12% in Newfoundland.

In contrast, seniors in Manitoba and Saskatchewan are the most likely seniors to live alone. In 1996, 34% of seniors in both Manitoba and Saskatchewan lived alone, compared with 30% in Quebec; 29% in British Columbia, Alberta, Nova Scotia, and Prince Edward Island; 28% in New Brunswick; 27% in Ontario; and just 21% in Newfoundland.

Family status of immigrant seniors

There is also variation in the living arrangements of senior immigrants and seniors born in Canada. In 1996, 75% of immigrant seniors were living with their family, compared with just 67% of those born in Canada. (Table 2.5)

Part of the reason for this difference is that immigrant seniors are more likely than their counterparts born in Canada to be living with their spouse. In 1996, 60% of immigrant seniors, compared with 57% of seniors born in Canada, lived with their husband, wife, or common-law partner.

Senior immigrants are also considerably more likely than their Canadian-born counterparts to live with members of their extended family. In 1996, 11% of immigrants aged 65 and over lived with members of their extended family, compared with only 6% of non-immigrant seniors.

In contrast, immigrant seniors are much less likely than Canadian-born seniors to live alone. In 1996, only 24% of immigrant seniors, versus 31% of those born in Canada, lived alone.

Differences in the family status of immigrant and non-immigrant seniors are most pronounced among women, particularly those not living with their husbands. Indeed, while about the same percentages of these women were living with their spouse in 1996, twice as many immigrant women aged 65 and over lived with members of their extended family as did their Canadian-born counterparts: 16% versus 8%. Senior immigrant women were also less likely than non-immigrant senior women to live alone: 32% versus 41%.

Family status of Aboriginal seniors

About the same shares of Aboriginal and non-Aboriginal seniors live with members of their family. In 1996, 71% of Aboriginal people aged 65 and over and 69% of non-Aboriginal seniors lived with their families. (Table 2.6)

Aboriginal seniors, however, are considerably less likely than their non-Aboriginal counterparts to be living with their spouse. In 1996, 44% of Aboriginal people aged 65 and over, versus 58% of non-Aboriginal seniors, lived with their husband, wife, or common-law partner.

On the other hand, Aboriginal seniors are far more likely than non-Aboriginal people aged 65 and over to be lone parents. In 1996, 12% of all Aboriginal people aged 65 and over were lone parents, compared with 4% of non-Aboriginal seniors. That year, 16% of all Aboriginal women aged 65 and over and 7% of senior Aboriginal men were lone parents.

Aboriginal seniors are also considerably more likely than non-Aboriginal seniors to live with members of their extended family. In 1996, 16% of all Aboriginal people aged 65 and over lived with members of their extended family, compared with 7% of non-Aboriginal seniors.

Senior Aboriginal women are the most likely to live with members of their extended family. In 1996, 19% of these women, versus 11% of senior Aboriginal men, lived with members of their extended family. Both senior Aboriginal women and men, though, were considerably more likely than their respective non-Aboriginal counterparts to live with their extended family that year.

Aboriginal seniors are also generally less likely than non-Aboriginal seniors to live alone. In 1996, 26% of Aboriginal seniors, compared with 29% of non-Aboriginal seniors, lived alone.

Among Aboriginal seniors, women are somewhat more likely than men to live alone: 29% versus 22% in 1996. Senior Aboriginal women, however, were less likely than their non-Aboriginal counterparts to live alone, whereas senior Aboriginal men were more likely than non-Aboriginal senior men to live alone.

Family status of Canadian veterans

As with other seniors, the majority of Canadian veterans live with their spouse. In 1995, 62% of all veterans lived with either their husband, wife, or common-law spouse, while 20% lived alone. (Chart 2.5)

Seniors looking after themselves

For the most part, Canadian seniors look after themselves. In 1996, 89% of all seniors devoted at least some time to unpaid housework activities on a weekly basis. That year, over 35% averaged 15 hours a week or more on such activities, while another 30% averaged between 5 and 14 hours a week. Overall, seniors devoted about the same amounts of time to household chores as people between the ages of 15 and 64 that year. (Table 2.7)

Chart 2.5

Living arrangements of veterans, 1995

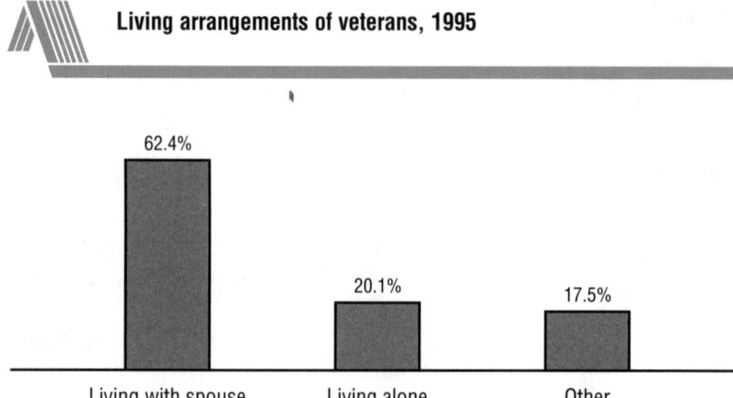

Source: Statistics Canada, 1995 General Social Survey.

Among seniors, women devote more time to household chores than do their male counterparts. In 1996, 92% of all women aged 65 and over, compared with 85% of men in this age range, spent at least some time per week on these activities. As well, almost half of senior women (49%) averaged 15 hours a week or more on household work activities, more than twice the figure for senior men (22%).

The proportion of seniors doing housework, however, declines with age, although the majority of even those aged 85 and over do some household chores. In 1996, 63% of those aged 85 and over spent at least some time per week on domestic work, as did 79% of those age 75 to 84 and 86% of 65- to 74-year-olds. As well, senior women were more likely than senior men to engage in these activities in all age ranges.

Seniors receiving and giving social support

While most seniors spend considerable amounts of time looking after themselves and their homes, the majority of seniors also get some help with household work and other personal chores. In 1996, 84% of all people aged 65 and over received some kind of assistance of this nature. That year, 67% received help with housework or household maintenance activities; 51% had help with transportation, grocery shopping, banking and bill-paying; 39% had someone check up on them via the telephone; 23% received some kind of emotional support; and 12% got help with personal care, including help received because of a long-term health condition or physical limitation. (Table 2.8)

Senior men and women are about as likely to receive help with these household or personal tasks. In 1996, 85% of men aged 65 and over and 83% of senior women got some kind of help at least once.

Chart 2.6

Percentage of seniors receiving home care services, 1997

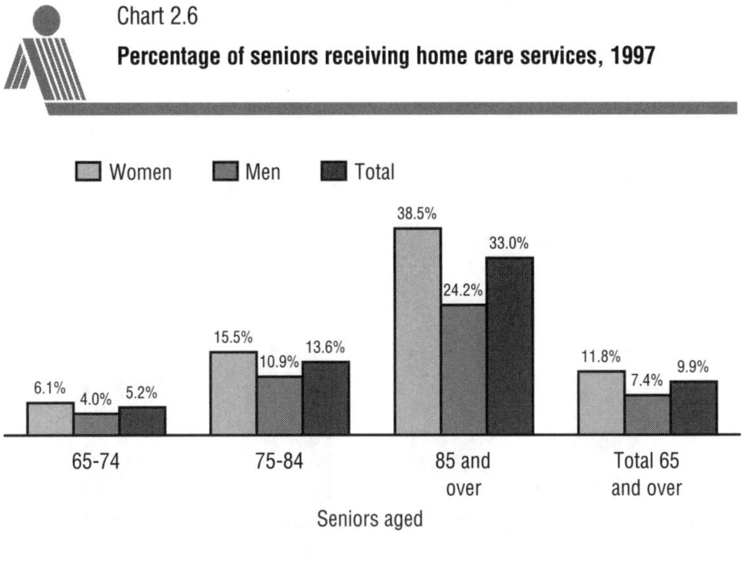

Source: Statistics Canada, National Population Health Survey.

There are differences, however, in the types of assistance senior men and women receive. Senior men were more likely than their female counterparts to get help with housework, while senior women were more likely to receive emotional support and to have someone check up on their well-being. Senior women were also slightly more likely than senior men to get help with transportation, shopping, banking and bill-paying, as well as with personal care activities.

Most seniors who get help receive it from family members or friends[2]. At the same time, however, a substantial proportion of seniors receive support from a home care service. In 1997, 10% of all people aged 65 and over received some assistance from such a organization. (Chart 2.6)

[2] *Source: Statistics Canada, 1991 Survey on Ageing and Independence.*

Senior women, especially those in older age ranges, are the most likely to receive help from a home care service. In 1997, 39% of women aged 85 and over got assistance from one of these services, compared with 16% of women aged 75 to 84 and just 6% of those aged 65 to 74.

Senior men aged 85 and over are also more likely than younger senior men to get help from a home care service. In 1997, 24% of men aged 85 and over, along with 11% of those aged 75 to 84 and 4% of men aged 65 to 74, received this kind of assistance; these figures, though, were all less than those for women in the same age group.

The provision of support to seniors in the home, however, is not a one-way street, as many seniors provide support to family and friends. In 1996, 37% of all seniors provided some sort of household or personal assistance to others. That year, 17% helped out with child care; 21% did housework or household maintenance; another 21% helped with shopping, transportation or financial activities; 27% provided emotional support; and 35% checked up on others by visiting or telephoning. (Table 2.9)

Indeed, many seniors spend considerable time on these types of activities. In 1996, 4% of seniors spent 5 to 14 hours per week on child care activities, while another 3% devoted an average of 15 hours or more per week to child care. Similarly, 7% of seniors spent at least 5 hours per week helping other seniors, a figure split evenly between those who spend 5 to 14 hours per week on such activities and those who averaged 15 hours or more per week[3].

Seniors living in an institution

While most seniors live in a private household, a substantial number live in an institution. In 1996, just over 250,000 people aged 65 and over, 7% of all seniors in Canada, lived in an institution. In fact, seniors were considerably more likely to live in an institution than those under the age of 65, among whom the figure was less than 1%. As a result, people aged 65 and over represented nearly 75% of all people in Canada living in an institution that year. (Table 2.10)

The proportion of the senior population living in an institution, however, has fallen in recent decades. In 1996, 7% of seniors were in an institution, down from 10% in 1971. (Chart 2.7)

Among seniors, those in older age ranges are more likely than their younger counterparts to reside in an institution. In 1996, 34% of people aged 85 and over, compared with 9% of those aged 75 to 84 and just 2% of 65- to 74-year-olds, lived in an institution. (Table 2.11)

[3] *Source: Statistics Canada, 1996 Census of Canada.*

Chart 2.7

Percentage of seniors living in an institution, 1971-1996

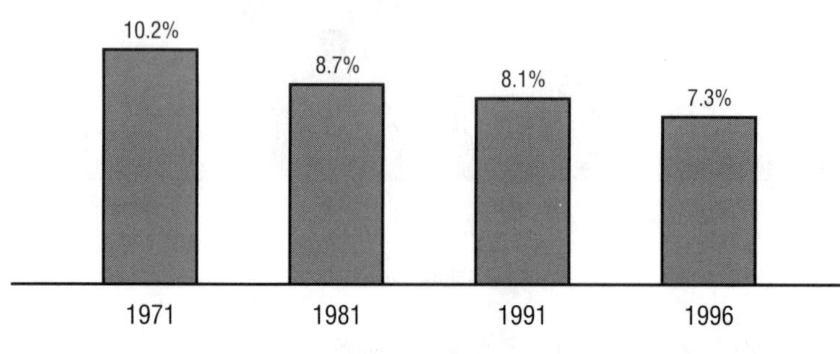

Source: Statistics Canada, Censuses of Canada.

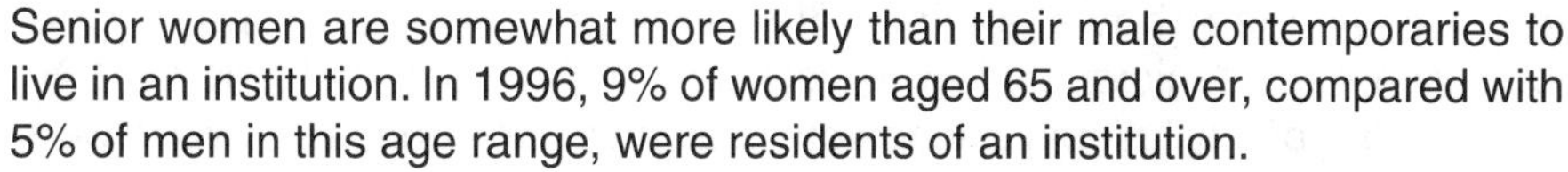

Senior women are somewhat more likely than their male contemporaries to live in an institution. In 1996, 9% of women aged 65 and over, compared with 5% of men in this age range, were residents of an institution.

Again, women in older age ranges are the most likely seniors to live in an institution. In 1996, 38% of women aged 85 and over, compared with 10% of women aged 75 to 84 and 2% of those aged 65 to 74, were in an institution.

Senior men in older age ranges are also far more likely than their younger counterparts to live in an institution. In 1996, 24% of men aged 85 and over, versus 7% of men aged 75 to 84 and 2% of those aged 65 to 74, were in an institution.

Men aged 85 and over, however, are much less likely than their female counterparts to live in an institution. In 1996, 24% of men in this age range were in an institution, compared with 38% of these women. In contrast, there was a much smaller difference in the likelihood of men and women aged 75 to 84 being in an institution that year, while there was almost no difference in the institutionalization rates of men and women aged 65 to 74.

Most seniors in institutions reside in special care homes for the elderly and chronically ill. In 1996, 6% of all people aged 65 and over lived in one of these institutions, while about a half a per cent resided in each of hospitals and religious institutions. (Table 2.10)

Seniors make up the large majority of those in special care homes. In 1996, over nine out of 10 residents of these institutions were aged 65 and over, while the figure was almost seven out of 10 in religious institutions and four out of 10 in hospitals. In contrast, seniors made up less than one in 10 of those in other institutions.

Seniors in older age ranges are especially likely to be in special care homes for the elderly and chronically ill. In 1996, 31% of all people aged 85 and over resided in such facilities, while 2% were in hospitals and 1% were in religious institutions.

Seniors across the country living in institutions

There is some variation in the proportion of seniors in different provinces in institutional care, although in no province do more than one out of 10 seniors live in an institution. In 1996, the proportion of seniors living in an institution ranged from 5% in British Columbia to 10% in Quebec. (Table 2.12)

The comparatively large percentage of Quebec seniors living in an institution results partly from the fact that many seniors in that province reside in a religious institution. In 1996, 15% of all institutionalized people aged 65 and over in Quebec lived in this type of facility, whereas the figure in the other provinces ranged from 7% in Prince Edward Island to less than 1% in British Columbia.

In all provinces, however, including Quebec, the large majority of institutionalized seniors reside in special care homes for the elderly. In 1996, around 90% of institutionalized seniors in all provinces outside Quebec were in these types of facilities, while the figure was 75% in Quebec.

At the same time, a number of institutionalized seniors in all provinces are in a hospital. In 1996, 11% of seniors living in an institution in Alberta were in a hospital, as were 10% of those in both Quebec and Newfoundland. In the other provinces, the figure ranged from 8% in Ontario, British Columbia, and Manitoba to 4% in Prince Edward Island.

Table 2.1

Family Status, 1996

	People aged					
	15-64			65 and over		
	Men	Women	Total	Men	Women	Total
	%					
Living with family:						
With husband or wife	49.5	51.4	50.4	74.6	42.7	56.5
With common-law partner	9.4	9.3	9.3	1.9	0.8	1.3
Lone parent	1.8	8.6	5.2	1.8	5.9	4.1
Child living with parents	21.2	16.3	18.7	0.1	0.1	0.1
Living with extended family members	2.9	2.4	2.6	2.6	10.3	7.4
Total living with family	84.8	88.0	86.4	82.1	59.8	69.4
Not living with family:						
Living alone	9.6	8.0	8.8	16.0	38.4	28.7
Living with non-relatives	5.7	4.0	4.8	1.9	1.7	1.8
Total not living with family	15.2	12.0	13.6	17.9	40.2	30.5
Total	100.0	100.0	100.0	100.0	100.0	100.0
Total population (000s)	9,545.9	9,708.3	19,254.2	1,408.6	1,843.7	3,252.3

Source: Statistics Canada, 1996 Census of Canada

Table 2.2

Family status of seniors, by age and sex, 1996

	Seniors aged								
	65-74			75-84			85 and over		
	Men	Women	Total	Men	Women	Total	Men	Women	Total
	%								
Living with family:									
With husband or wife	77.4	53.8	64.6	71.9	30.4	47.2	55.0	10.8	25.6
With common-law partner	2.3	1.1	1.7	1.2	0.5	0.8	0.8	0.2	0.4
Lone parent	1.6	5.9	3.9	1.9	5.7	4.2	3.3	7.3	6.0
Child living with parents	0.1	0.1	0.1	--	--	--	--	--	--
Living with extended family members	2.7	7.6	5.4	4.6	12.4	9.3	10.3	21.9	18.0
Total living with family	84.2	68.4	75.7	79.6	49.1	61.4	69.4	40.2	50.0
Not living with family:									
Living alone	13.8	29.8	22.4	18.6	49.2	36.9	28.6	57.8	48.0
Living with non-relatives	2.0	1.8	1.9	1.7	1.7	1.7	20.0	2.0	2.0
Total not living with family	15.9	31.5	24.3	20.4	50.9	38.6	30.6	59.8	50.0
Total	100.0	100.0	100.0	100.0	100.0	100.0	100.0	100.0	100.0
Total population (000s)	923.9	1,088.3	2,012.2	411.0	609.6	1,020.6	73.6	145.8	219.4

Source: Statistics Canada, 1996 Census of Canada.

Table 2.3

Marital status of seniors, by age and sex, 1996

	Married	Separated	Divorced	Widowed	Single, never married	Total	Total population
			%				000s
Seniors aged:							
65-74							
Men	79.2	2.3	4.6	7.4	6.4	100.0	943.4
Women	55.0	2.1	5.5	31.6	5.8	100.0	1,118.6
Total	66.0	2.2	5.1	20.6	6.1	100.0	2,061.9
75-84							
Men	71.4	2.0	2.6	17.8	6.1	100.0	444.2
Women	30.4	1.3	2.6	58.2	7.4	100.0	684.7
Total	46.6	1.6	2.6	42.3	6.9	100.0	1,128.8
85 and over							
Men	50.9	1.9	1.6	38.6	7.0	100.0	100.3
Women	9.5	0.6	1.1	79.2	9.7	100.0	236.8
Total	21.8	1.0	1.2	67.1	8.9	100.0	337.1
Total 65 and over							
Men	74.9	2.2	3.8	12.7	6.4	100.0	1,487.8
Women	41.4	1.6	4.0	46.1	6.8	100.0	2,040.0
Total	55.6	1.9	3.9	32.0	6.6	100.0	3,527.9

Source: Statistics Canada, 1996 Census of Canada.

Table 2.4

Family status of seniors, by province, 1996

	Living with family			Not living with family		
	Living with immediate family	Living with extended family	Total with family	Living alone	Living with non-relatives	Total
	%					
Newfoundland	65.6	11.8	77.4	21.1	1.5	100.0
Prince Edward Island	60.3	8.5	68.8	28.8	2.3	100.0
Nova Scotia	59.2	9.1	68.3	29.4	2.3	100.0
New Brunswick	61.1	8.5	69.6	28.1	2.3	100.0
Quebec	60.4	7.6	68.0	29.7	2.3	100.0
Ontario	63.1	8.0	71.1	27.3	1.6	100.0
Manitoba	59.4	5.3	64.7	34.1	1.1	100.0
Saskatchewan	61.3	3.8	65.1	33.5	1.4	100.0
Alberta	63.3	6.3	69.6	28.6	1.7	100.0
British Columbia	62.8	6.7	69.5	28.6	1.9	100.0
Canada	62.0	7.4	69.4	28.7	1.8	100.0

Source: Statistics Canada, 1996 Census of Canada.

Table 2.5

Family status of immigrant and non-immigrant seniors, 1996

	Immigrant seniors			Non-immigrant seniors		
	Men	Women	Total	Men	Women	Total
	%					
Living with family:						
With husband or wife	77.8	43.6	58.9	73.3	42.4	55.6
With common-law partner	1.3	0.5	0.9	2.2	0.9	1.4
Lone parent	1.9	6.3	4.3	1.7	5.8	4.0
Child living with parents	--	0.1	0.1	0.1	0.1	0.1
Living with extended family members	4.2	16.1	10.8	3.4	8.1	6.1
Total living with family	85.3	66.5	75.0	80.7	57.3	67.3
Not living with family:						
Living alone	13.1	32.1	23.6	17.2	40.8	30.7
Living with non-relatives	1.5	1.4	1.4	2.1	1.8	2.0
Total not living with family	14.7	33.5	25.0	19.3	42.7	32.7
Total	100.0	100.0	100.0	100.0	100.0	100.0
Total population (000s)	402.1	494.9	897.0	1,004.0	1,343.9	2,347.9

Source: Statistics Canada, 1996 Census of Canada.

Table 2.6

Family status of Aboriginal and non-Aboriginal seniors, 1996

	Aboriginal seniors			Non-Aboriginal seniors		
	Men	Women	Total	Men	Women	Total
	%					
Living with family:						
With husband or wife	51.8	30.6	40.2	74.8	42.8	56.7
With common-law partner	4.4	2.6	3.4	1.9	0.8	1.3
Lone parent	6.8	16.1	11.9	1.8	5.8	4.1
Child living with parents	0.2	0.2	0.2	0.1	0.1	0.1
Living with extended family members	11.1	19.4	15.6	3.6	10.3	7.4
Total living with family	74.3	68.8	71.3	82.1	59.8	69.4
Not living with family:						
Living alone	22.2	28.5	25.7	16.0	38.5	28.7
Living with non-relatives	3.4	2.7	3.0	1.9	1.7	1.8
Total not living with family	25.7	31.2	28.7	17.9	40.2	30.5
Total	100.0	100.0	100.0	100.0	100.0	100.0
Total population (000s)	12.7	15.3	28.0	1,395.9	1,828.4	3,224.3

Source: Statistics Canada, 1996 Census of Canada.

Table 2.7

Percentage of people spending time on unpaid housework, by number of hours per week, 1996

	Number of hours per week							
	None	Less than 5	5-14	15-29	30-59	60 or more	Total spending time on unpaid housework	Total
	%							
People aged:								
15-64								
Men	14.7	31.9	33.5	13.6	4.7	1.6	85.4	100.0
Women	6.2	16.4	28.9	24.2	16.4	8.0	93.8	100.0
Total	10.4	24.1	31.2	18.9	10.6	4.8	89.6	100.0
65-74								
Men	17.1	17.4	28.6	20.4	13.0	3.4	82.9	100.0
Women	10.9	9.2	23.6	25.4	23.9	7.1	89.2	100.0
Total	13.7	13.0	25.9	23.1	18.9	5.4	86.3	100.0
75-84								
Men	24.9	19.0	26.5	16.7	10.1	2.7	75.1	100.0
Women	18.6	14.6	26.4	20.7	15.4	4.2	81.4	100.0
Total	21.2	16.4	26.4	19.1	13.3	3.6	78.8	100.0
85 and over								
Men	40.5	19.7	20.8	11.5	5.6	1.8	59.4	100.0
Women	34.8	19.4	22.8	13.6	7.5	1.8	65.2	100.0
Total	36.7	19.6	22.1	12.9	6.9	1.8	63.3	100.0
Total 65 and over								
Men	15.4	30.1	32.8	14.3	5.6	1.8	84.6	100.0
Women	7.7	15.7	28.1	24.0	17.0	7.6	92.4	100.0
Total	11.4	22.7	30.4	19.3	11.4	4.8	88.6	100.0

Source: Statistics Canada, 1996 Census of Canada.

Table 2.8

Percentage of seniors who received assistance with household or personal tasks or chores in the past 12 months, 1996

	Men	Women	Total
		%	
Received help with[1]:			
Housework[2]	74.7	61.0	67.0
Shopping, transportation, banking or bill paying	49.9	52.0	51.1
Child care	1.7	1.6	1.6
Personal care[3]	10.0	13.2	11.9
Checking up by visiting or telephoning	30.0	45.7	38.9
Emotional support	18.4	26.0	22.7
Any of the above	84.6	83.2	83.8

1 *Includes assistance from people living with the senior or outside their home.*
2 *Includes meal preparation and clean-up, house cleaning, laundry and sewing, and home maintenance and outside work.*
3 *Includes help received because of a health condition or physical limitation.*
Source: Statistics Canada, 1996 General Social Survey.

Table 2.9

Percentage of seniors who provided assistance with household or personal tasks or chores in the past 12 months, 1996

	Men	Women	Total
		%	
Gave help with:			
Child care	15.4	18.2	17.0
Housework[1]	22.7	19.1	20.7
Shopping, transportation, banking or bill paying	23.4	19.3	21.1
Personal care[2]	3.7	4.5	4.2
Checking up by visiting or telephoning	29.4	39.7	35.3
Emotional support	19.8	32.2	27.3
Any of the above	38.0	37.1	37.4

1 *Includes meal preparation and clean-up, house cleaning, laundry and sewing, and home maintenance and outside work.*
2 *Includes assistance provided to persons with a health condition or physical limitation.*
Source: Statistics Canada, 1996 General Social Survey.

Table 2.10

Population living in an institution, by age, 1996

	Percentage of total population living in					
	Hospitals	Special care homes	Religious institutions	Other	Total in institutions	Total population in institutions
			%			000s
People aged:						
Under 15	--	--	--	--	0.1	2.8
15-24	0.1	--	--	0.2	0.3	11.6
25-54	0.2	0.1	--	0.1	0.4	54.4
55-64	0.2	0.4	0.2	--	0.8	19.4
65-74	0.3	1.4	0.3	--	2.1	43.1
75-84	0.8	7.4	0.6	--	8.9	99.4
85 and over	2.1	30.8	0.9	--	33.8	111.9
Total 65 and over	0.6	6.2	0.4	--	7.3	254.4
Total population (000s)	58.2	233.9	23.9	26.4	342.6	342.6

Source: Statistics Canada, 1996 Census of Canada.

Table 2.11

Seniors living in an institution, by age and sex, 1996

	Percentage of total population living in			
	Hospitals	Special care homes	Religious institutions	Total in institutions
		%		
Seniors aged:				
65-74				
Men	0.4	1.3	0.2	1.9
Women	0.3	1.6	0.4	2.3
Total	0.3	1.4	0.3	2.1
75-84				
Men	0.9	5.5	0.3	6.7
Women	0.7	8.8	0.9	10.3
Total	0.8	7.4	0.6	8.9
85 and over				
Men	1.9	22.0	0.4	24.3
Women	2.2	34.4	1.1	37.7
Total	2.1	30.8	0.9	33.8
Total 65 and over				
Men	0.6	3.9	0.2	4.8
Women	0.6	7.8	0.7	9.1
Total	0.6	6.2	0.4	7.3

Source: Statistics Canada, 1996 Census of Canada.

Table 2.12

Percentage of seniors living in an institution, by province, 1996

	Percentage of population aged 65 and over living in				
	Hospitals	Special care homes	Religious institutions	Total in institutions	Total number of seniors in an institution
			%		
Newfoundland	0.6	5.7	0.3	6.7	3,935
Prince Edward Island	0.3	7.4	0.6	8.4	1,440
Nova Scotia	0.4	5.3	0.3	6.0	7,090
New Brunswick	0.4	5.8	0.4	6.7	6,225
Quebec	1.0	7.3	1.4	9.7	82,660
Ontario	0.5	5.8	0.2	6.4	86,040
Manitoba	0.5	5.9	0.3	6.6	10,005
Saskatchewan	0.3	6.7	0.2	7.2	10,430
Alberta	0.8	6.9	0.1	7.8	20,675
British Columbia	0.4	5.0	--	5.4	25,685
Canada	0.6	6.2	0.4	7.3	254,365

Source: Statistics Canada, 1996 Census of Canada.

Housing and Household Facilities

Homeownership rates high

A substantial majority of seniors own their homes. Indeed, in 1997, 68% of all households headed by someone aged 65 and over owned their home. The proportion of senior households owning their home, however, was less than the figure for households headed by people aged either 55 to 64 (78%) or 45 to 54 (75%), while it was higher than that for households headed by someone under age 35 (42%). At the same time, senior households were about as likely to be homeowners as households headed by someone aged 35 to 44 (67%). (Chart 3.1)

In addition, the proportion of seniors households owning their homes has risen somewhat in the past decade. In 1997, 68% were homeowners, up from 64% in 1988[1].

Seniors living in a family are more likely than those who live alone to be homeowners. In 1997, 84% of families headed by someone aged 65 and over lived in an owner-occupied dwelling, compared with 50% of unattached seniors. (Table 3.1)

Among unattached seniors, men are slightly more likely than women to be homeowners. In 1997, 54% of unattached men aged 65 and over owned their home, while the figure was 49% among their female counterparts.

Most senior homeowners mortgage-free

The large majority of senior homeowners have paid off their mortgage. In 1997, almost nine out of 10 home-owning households headed by a senior were mortgage-free. That year, 59% of all senior households were mortgage-free homeowners, while only 10% were homeowners with a mortgage. (Chart 3.1)

Senior households are more likely than householders in all other age groups to be mortgage-free homeowners. In 1997, 59% of all households headed by a senior owned their home outright, compared with 52% of households with head aged 55 to 64, 33% of those with head aged 45 to 54, 18% of those with head aged 35 to 44, and just 8% of those with head under age 35.

As well, among home-owning senior households, the large majority of both families and unattached individuals have paid off their mortgage. In 1997, over eight out of 10 home-owning families headed by a senior, and nine out of 10 of unattached senior homeowners, had paid off their mortgages. That year, 71% of all households with a senior head, and 45% of all unattached seniors, owned homes on which the mortgage was paid off. (Table 3.1)

---

[1] *Source: Statistics Canada, Catalogue no. 13-218-XPB.*

There is a similar pattern for both male and female unattached senior homeowners, as about nine out of 10 of each have paid off their mortgages. In 1997, 48% of all unattached men aged 65 and over were mortgage-free homeowners, as were 44% of their female counterparts.

Chart 3.1

Percentage of households owning their homes, by age of head, 1997

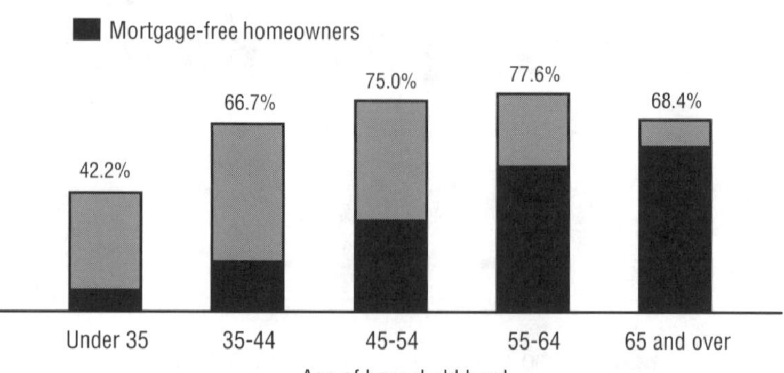

Source: Statistics Canada, Catalogue no. 13-218-XPB.

Senior renters

While the majority of seniors live in owner-occupied homes, close to one in three seniors are renters. In 1997, 32% of all households headed by a senior lived in a rented dwelling, compared with 22% of households headed by someone aged 55 to 64, 25% of those with head aged 45 to 54, 33% of those with head aged 35 to 44, and 58% of those with head under age 35. (Chart 3.2)

Among seniors, those who live alone are more much likely than those who live in a family to rent. In 1997, 50% of all unattached seniors lived in rented accommodations, versus only 16% of families with head aged 65 and over. In addition, among unattached seniors, women were somewhat more likely than their male counterparts to rent that year: 51% versus 46%. (Table 3.1)

Chart 3.2

Percentage of households renting their homes, by age of head, 1997

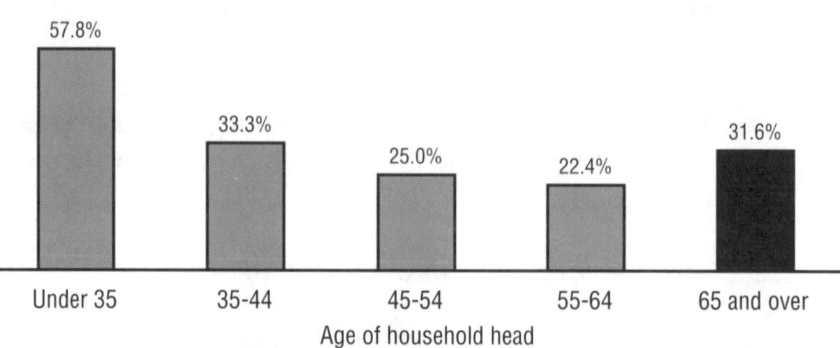

Source: Statistics Canada, Catalogue no. 13-218-XPB.

Seniors who rent, though, generally pay lower rents, on average, than other households. In 1997, senior renters paid an average rent of $527, compared with almost $600 for households with head under age 25 and well over $600 for households with head between the ages of 25 and 64. (Table 3.2)

However, because the incomes of senior renters are also relatively small, these seniors actually pay a higher proportion of their total income on rent than most other renter households. In 1997, rent represented 29% of the total household income of senior renters, compared with 25% of that of renter households with head aged 55 to 64 and only 22% of that of these households with head between the ages of 25 and 54. Households with head under age 25, who devoted 30% of their total income to rent, were the only age group which spent a greater proportion of their total income on rent than seniors that year.

Among senior renter households, family units pay more in rent, on average, than single-person households. In 1997, renter families headed by someone aged 65 and over paid an average rent of $667, compared with $464 for their unattached seniors counterparts. (Table 3.3)

Again, because unattached senior renters have much lower incomes, on average, than senior families that rent, unattached seniors pay a considerably higher

Chart 3.3

Percentage of households living in dwellings requiring repairs, 1997

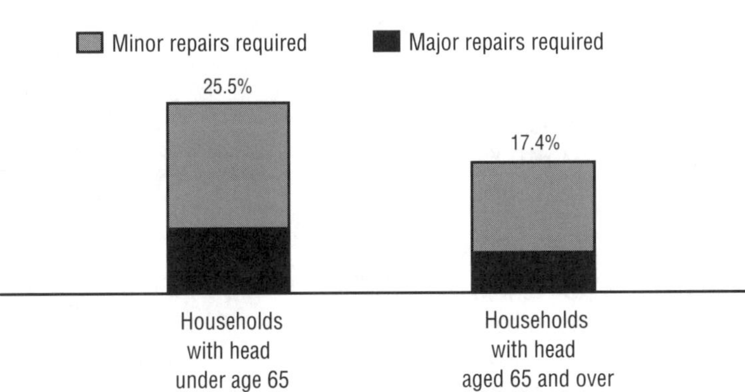

Source: Statistics Canada, Household Facilities and Equipment Survey.

Chart 3.4

Average number of rooms per person, by household type, 1997

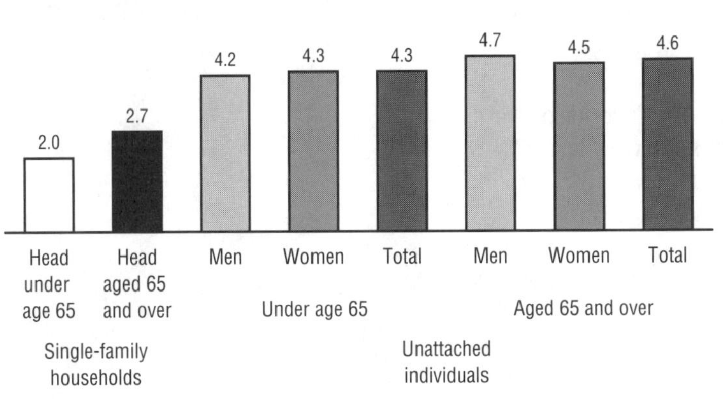

Source: Statistics Canada, Household Facilities and Equipment Survey.

percentage of their income on rent than families. In 1997, rent represented 32% of the income of unattached seniors, compared with only 24% of that of renter families headed by someone aged 65 and over.

Similarly among unattached senior renters, men paid more in rent than women in 1997: $515 versus $441. However, because the incomes of these women were much lower, on average, their rent represented 33% of their income, compared with 28% of that of their male counterparts.

The homes of seniors needing repairs

Seniors are generally less likely than younger people to live in homes needing repairs other than regular maintenance. In 1997, 17% of the dwellings of all households headed by a senior required either major or minor repairs, compared with 26% of households headed by someone between the ages of 15 and 64. (Chart 3.3)

As well, most of the homes of seniors that need repair only require minor work. In 1997, 12% of senior households required minor repairs, while just 5% needed major work. Again both figures were below those for households with head under age 65.

Families with head aged 65 and over (18%) were about as likely as unattached seniors (17%) to live in dwellings needing repair in 1997. Among unattached seniors, though, men were somewhat more likely than their female counterparts to live in housing that needed repairs: 20% compared with 16%. Whatever the family type, however, senior households were considerably less likely than the comparable non-senior households to live in dwellings requiring repairs. (Table 3.4)

The dwellings of home-owning seniors, particularly those belonging to unattached seniors, are also somewhat more likely to be in need of repairs than those of senior renters. For example, the dwellings of 21% of unattached senior homeowners required repairs in 1997, compared with 13% of those of unattached senior renters. (Table 3.5)

Living space

The homes of seniors have more living space, on average, than those of younger people. In 1997, the dwellings of families headed by a senior had an average of 2.7 rooms per person, compared with 2.0 rooms per person in the homes of families headed by someone between the ages of 15 and 64. (Chart 3.4)

Similarly, unattached seniors lived in dwellings which had an average of 4.6 rooms per person in 1997, compared with a figure of 4.3 for unattached people under age 65. Unattached senior men, though, had slightly more living space than their female counterparts: 4.7 rooms per dwelling versus 4.5.

Household amenities

Almost all seniors in Canada live in homes which have basic household facilities such as baths, flush toilets, refrigerators, and telephones. Indeed, close to 100% of the homes of both families headed by seniors and unattached individuals aged 65 and over had these facilities in 1997. (Table 3.6)

Relatively large shares of the senior population also have many other household conveniences in their homes. For example, in 1997, 87% of families headed by a senior had an automatic washing machine, while 86% had a microwave oven, 85% had a clothes dryer, 70% had a freezer, 52% had a dishwasher, and 48% had a gas barbecue, figures which were about the same as those for families headed by someone under age 65.

Unattached seniors are also about as likely as unattached individuals under age 65 to have most of these amenities. The shares of unattached seniors with these amenities in 1997, however, were all 20 to 30 percentage points lower than those of families headed by a senior. Unattached senior women and men were also about as likely to have most of these household conveniences; these women, though, were more likely than their male counterparts to have a freezer or microwave oven, while men were more likely to own a gas barbecue.

Seniors are also generally more likely than younger people to own air conditioners. In 1997, 36% of family households headed by someone aged 65 and over and 27% of unattached seniors had air conditioners. In comparison, the figures were 31% among non-senior families and 21% among unattached individuals under age 65.

Substantial numbers of seniors also have standard safety equipment such as smoke detectors and portable fire extinguishers. In 1997, almost all senior families (96%) and unattached seniors (95%) had smoke detectors in their homes, while 62% of family households headed by a senior, and 38% of unattached seniors, had a fire extinguisher.

Vehicle ownership

Most families headed by seniors own a car or other vehicle. In 1997, 90% of these families owned at least one vehicle, about the same figure as for families headed by someone under age 65 (91%). As well, over one in three senior families (35%) owned at least two vehicles that year. (Table 3.7)

In contrast, only about half of unattached seniors own a vehicle. In 1997, just 51% of unattached individuals aged 65 and over owned at least one vehicle, compared with 68% of unattached people under age 65.

Among unattached seniors, men are more likely than women to have a vehicle. In 1997, 69% of unattached men aged 65 and over, compared with 45% of their female counterparts, had at least one vehicle.

Table 3.1

Housing tenure of seniors, by family status, 1997

	Families with head aged 65 and over	Unattached individuals aged 65 and over		
		Men	Women	Total
		%		
Tenure:				
Owned				
With mortgage	13.1	6.7	5.2	5.5
Without mortgage	70.7	47.7	43.7	44.7
Total owned	83.8	54.4	48.8	50.2
Rented	16.2	45.6	51.2	49.8
Total	100.0	100.0	100.0	100.0
Total number of households (000s)	1,246.6	261.2	790.2	1,051.4

Source: Statistics Canada, Household Facilities and Equipment Survey.

Table 3.2

Average rent paid by renter households, by age of head, 1997

	Average monthly rent	Total household income	Rent as a % of total income
	$		
Households with head aged:			
Under 25	595	23,793	30
25-34	628	34,280	22
35-44	647	35,297	22
45-54	695	37,889	22
55-64	641	30,745	25
65 and over	527	21,820	29
Total	655	31,439	25

Source: Statistics Canada, Catalogue no. 13-218-XPB.

Table 3.3

Average rent paid by senior renter households, 1997

	Average monthly rent	Total household income	Rent as a % of total income
	$		
Family households with head aged 65 and over	667	33,367	24
Unattached seniors			
Men	515	22,063	28
Women	441	16,026	33
Total	464	17,387	32

Source: Statistics Canada, Household Facilities and Equipment Survey.

Table 3.4

Percentage of families and unattached individuals living in dwellings needing repairs, 1997

	Families with head aged		Unattached individuals aged					
			15-64			65 and over		
	15-64	65 and over	Men	Women	Total	Men	Women	Total
	%							
Dwellings needing repairs:								
Major repairs	8.6	6.1	9.7	8.0	9.0	7.1	4.1	4.8
Minor repairs	16.4	11.8	19.5	17.3	18.6	12.8	12.0	12.2
Total needing repairs	25.0	17.9	29.2	25.3	27.5	19.9	16.1	17.0
Regular maintenance only	75.0	82.0	70.8	74.6	72.4	80.2	83.9	83.0
Total	100.0	100.0	100.0	100.0	100.0	100.0	100.0	100.0
Total number of households (000s)	6,920	1,222	1,070	793	1,863	261	790	1,051

Source: Statistics Canada, Household Facilities and Equipment Survey.

Table 3.5

Percentage of senior households living in dwellings needing repairs, by tenure, 1997

	Families with head aged 65 and over		Unattached individuals aged 65 and over					
			Men		Women		Total	
	Owned	Rented	Owned	Rented	Owned	Rented	Owned	Rented
	%							
Dwellings needing repairs:								
Major repairs	6.3	5.2	9.2	4.6	6.3	2.0	7.1	2.6
Minor repairs	12.1	10.4	13.2	12.3	14.7	9.4	14.3	10.1
Total needing repairs	18.4	16.6	22.4	16.9	21.0	11.4	21.4	12.7
Regular maintenance only	81.5	84.4	77.7	83.1	79.0	88.6	78.6	87.4
Total	100.0	100.0	100.0	100.0	100.0	100.0	100.0	100.0

Source: Statistics Canada, Household Facilities and Equipment Survey.

Table 3.6

Percentage of families and unattached individuals with selected household amenities, 1997

	Families with head aged		Unattached individuals aged					
			15-64			65 and over		
	15-64	65 and over	Men	Women	Total	Men	Women	Total
	%							
Bath facilities	99.9	99.8	99.0	99.7	99.3	99.5	99.7	99.7
Flush toilet	99.9	99.8	99.1	99.7	99.3	99.6	99.8	99.7
Refrigerator	99.8	100.0	99.4	99.5	99.5	99.6	99.6	99.6
Automatic washing machine	88.2	87.3	50.1	56.2	52.7	55.5	56.4	56.1
Clothes dryer	86.8	85.2	49.0	54.0	51.1	51.5	53.9	53.3
Dishwasher	58.1	51.6	25.6	29.2	27.1	24.1	26.0	25.5
Freezer	64.9	70.3	23.6	27.5	25.3	38.2	43.0	41.8
Microwave oven	91.9	86.3	72.3	78.8	75.0	64.0	71.4	69.5
Gas barbecue	68.3	48.1	30.1	25.2	28.0	22.2	14.0	16.1
Air conditioner	30.8	36.1	19.4	23.2	21.1	24.5	27.4	26.6
Smoke detector	97.0	95.7	92.4	96.3	94.0	93.1	95.2	94.7
Fire extinguisher	59.7	61.8	35.5	32.8	34.3	44.4	35.2	37.5
Telephone	99.1	99.9	94.3	97.7	95.7	98.5	99.2	99.1
Total number of households (000s)	6,920	1,222	1,070	793	1,863	261	790	1,051

Sources: Statistics Canada, Catalogue no. 13-218-XPB; and Household Facilities and Equipment Survey.

Table 3.7

Percentage of families and unattached individuals owning vehicles, 1997

	Families with head aged		Unattached individuals aged					
			15-64			65 and over		
	15-64	65 and over	Men	Women	Total	Men	Women	Total
				%				
Households with:								
At least one automobile	79.6	80.3	53.4	60.0	56.2	55.4	42.5	45.7
Vans or trucks	41.7	28.3	24.4	7.5	17.2	20.7	5.0	8.9
Total with vehicles								
One	37.5	55.0	58.1	60.1	58.9	58.3	40.6	45.0
Two or more	53.7	34.7	12.2	5.0	9.1	10.5	4.4	5.9
Total	91.2	89.7	70.3	65.1	68.0	68.8	45.0	50.9
Total without vehicles	8.8	10.3	29.7	34.9	32.0	31.2	55.0	49.1
Total	100.0	100.0	100.0	100.0	100.0	100.0	100.0	100.0
Total number of households (000s)	6,920	1,222	1,070	793	1,863	261	790	1,051

Sources: Statistics Canada, Catalogue no. 13-218-XPB; and Household Facilities and Equipment Survey.

Health

Increasing life expectancy among seniors

The remaining life expectancy of Canadian seniors has risen substantially over the course of this century. As of 1996, a 65-year-old person had an estimated remaining life expectancy of 18.4 years, roughly a half a year more than in 1991, three years more than in 1971, and five years more than in 1921. (Table 4.1)

As in other age groups, senior women have a longer remaining life expectancy than senior men. A woman aged 65 in 1996, for instance, could expect to live, on average, another 20.2 years, almost four years longer than the figure for a man aged 65 (16.3).

This difference reflects the fact that the remaining life expectancy of senior women has increased much faster than that of senior men during most of the period since the early 1920s. Between 1921 and 1981, the average life expectancy of a 65-year-old woman rose by over five years, compared with an increase of less than two years for her male counterpart.

This trend, however, has reversed somewhat in the last decade and a half. Between 1981 and 1991, the life expectancy of both senior men and women increased by just over a year, while in the 1991 to 1996 period, the average remaining life expectancy of a 65-year-old man rose by a half a year, compared with an increase of just 0.2 years for women aged 65.

The remaining life expectancy of seniors, of course, declines with age. Still, someone aged 90 in 1996 could expect to live close to 5 more years, on average, while the figure was 6.6 years for those aged 85 and almost 9 years for those aged 80. There were also gains in the average remaining life expectancy of seniors at all ages in the first half of the 1990s, with the largest gains occurring among younger seniors. (Table 4.2)

Death rates among seniors down

Gains in life expectancy among Canadian seniors reflect long-term declines in death rates among people in this age group. Between 1980 and 1996, the age-standardized[1] death rate among people aged 65 and over fell 12%, from just over 5,000 deaths per 100,000 seniors to 4,430. (Table 4.3)

Among seniors, death rates are considerably higher among men than among women. In 1996, there were over 5,600 deaths for every 100,000 men aged 65 and over, compared with just over 3,600 per 100,000 senior women. Between 1980 and 1996, however, the age-standardized death rates for both senior men and women fell 12%.

[1] *These figures have been age-standardized to the 1991 Canadian population.*

Death rates have also fallen among seniors in all age ranges, although declines have been greater among younger seniors than those in older age groups. Between 1980 and 1996, the annual death rate among people aged 65 to 74 declined 20%, while the figure was down 15% among those aged 75 to 84 and 5% among those aged 85 and over. (Table 4.4)

Heart disease and cancer main causes of death among seniors

Heart disease and cancer account for over half the deaths of Canadian seniors. In 1996, 30% of all deaths of people aged 65 and over were attributed to heart disease and 26% were from cancer. Of the remaining deaths of seniors, 11% were from respiratory diseases, 9% were from strokes, while 24% were attributed to all other diseases and conditions combined. (Table 4.3)

There have, however, been considerable differences in the direction of the long-term trends in the main causes of death among seniors. The age-standardized death rate due to heart disease among seniors, for example, was 34% lower in 1996 than in 1980, whereas the figure for cancer rose 9% in the same period.

There was a similar pattern in the age-standardized death rates of seniors due to strokes and respiratory diseases. Between 1980 and 1996, there was a 34% decline in the death rate among seniors as a result of strokes, while there was an 18% increase in deaths due to respiratory diseases.

Heart disease and cancer are also the leading causes of death of both senior men and women, although death rates from both are much higher among senior men than senior women.

The death rate from cancer among senior women, however, has risen somewhat faster than that of their male counterparts in the past decade and a half. Between 1980 and 1996, the age-standardized death rate from cancer among senior women rose 12%, compared with a 9% increase among senior men.

There is also considerable variation in the main causes of death among seniors in different age groups. Heart disease, for example, is very much a disease of older seniors. In 1996, the death rate from heart disease among people aged 85 and over was two and half times that of cancer, whereas cancer was the leading cause of death among 65- to 74-year-olds. (Table 4.4)

Lung cancer rates increasing among seniors

Much of the increase in the overall cancer death rate among seniors is accounted for by increases in deaths from lung cancer, particularly among senior women. In fact, the age-specific death rate due to lung cancer for women in each age group over age 60 in 1998[2] was more than double the figure for women in these age groups in 1980. (Table 4.5)

[2] *The data in this section are for 1996 as opposed to the previous section which only has cancer data for 1994. The National Cancer Institute of Canada provides projections regarding cancer incidence and mortality in Canada in 1996. Mortality figures for other diseases, however, are only available through 1994; as a result, in order to put cancer deaths in the context of other causes, only 1994 figures are used in the previous section.*

The health of seniors living in institutions

Not surprisingly, many seniors living in an institution[1] have health problems, although even these seniors generally rate their health in positive terms. In 1995, 43% of seniors living in an institution said their health was either good, very good, or excellent, while 34% said their health was only fair and 22% said it was poor.

Almost all seniors living in an institution, however, have a chronic health condition. In 1995, 95% of these seniors had such a condition. That year, 45% had arthritis or rheumatism, 27% had a chronic heart condition, 24% had high blood pressure, 22% suffered from the effects of a stroke, 19% had osteoporosis or brittle bones, 14% had chronic digestive problems, 13% had diabetes, 13% had chronic bronchitis, emphysema or other lung condition, and 8% suffered from partial or complete paralysis.

As well, about 80% of institutionalized seniors reported some level of activity restriction because of a long-term health condition in 1995. That year, 72% needed help with personal care activities such as bathing, dressing, and eating, while almost half needed help getting in and out of bed (49%), getting in and out of a chair (46%), or moving about the facility (47%).

Many seniors living in an institution have memory problems. In 1995, 66% had at least some difficulty remembering things and 21% were unable to remember anything at all.

In addition, 28% of all people aged 65 and over in an institution could not see well enough to read, even with corrective lenses. At the same time, about a quarter of these seniors had hearing problems (26%).

Seniors in institutions, though, see a doctor regularly. In 1995, 96% saw a doctor at least once a year. That year, 26% saw a doctor at least once a week and 37% saw one at least once a month. As well, 91% saw a nurse at least once a week, while 14% saw a therapist at least once a week and 22% saw one at least once a month.

Almost all institutionalized seniors also take some form of medication. In 1995, 96% of these seniors had taken at least one form of medication in the two days prior to the survey. Indeed, 88% had taken two or more medications in the two days prior to the survey and 38% had taken more than five different types of medication in this period.

---

[1] *Includes residents of long-term health care facilities such as hospitals, nursing homes, and residential care facilities for persons with disabilities; but excludes those in long-term health care facilities on military bases, in correctional institutions, or on Indian reserves.*

Senior men, however, are still considerably more likely than their female counterparts to die from lung cancer. The estimated death rate from lung cancer among men aged 80 and over in 1998 was over three times the figure for women in this age range, while estimated rates for men aged 60 to 69 and 70 to 79 were both around twice those of their female counterparts.

Increases in the lung cancer death rate among seniors reflect, in part, increases in the number of new cases of this disease among people aged 60 and over. This is particularly the case for senior women. The estimated number of new cases of this disease diagnosed for every 100,000 women in both the 70 to 79 and 80 and over age ranges in 1998 were almost three times higher than the figures in 1980, while the 1998 rate among women aged 60 to 69 was more than twice that in 1980. (Table 4.6)

As with death rates from lung cancer, however, senior men in all age ranges are still considerably more likely than their female counterparts to develop lung cancer. Among those aged 80 and over, for example, the estimated number of new lung cancer cases for every 100,000 men in 1998 was almost three times greater than the figure for women in this age range.

Other forms of cancer among seniors

There are also differences in long-term trends in other forms of cancer among seniors. There have, for instance, been substantial increases in deaths attributed to prostate cancer among senior men, especially those aged 80 and over. Indeed, the estimated death rate from prostate cancer among men aged 80 and over was higher than that for lung cancer in 1998. (Table 4.5)

There has been an even more dramatic rise in the number of newly diagnosed cases of prostate cancer among senior men since the early 1980s. As a result, prostate cancer is now the leading cause of new cases of cancer among men in all age groups over age 60. (Table 4.6)

Part of the rise in the number of newly-diagnosed cases of prostate cancer among senior men reflects increases in the use of screening and other techniques for earlier detection of this disease. As well, increases in the number of new cases of prostate cancer among senior men are substantially greater than increases in deaths from this disease among these men. This suggests that prostate cancer is either being detected earlier or treated more effectively[3].

There have also been increases in death rates from breast cancer among senior women aged 70 and over in the past two decades. In fact, breast cancer was the leading cause of cancer deaths among women aged 80 and over in 1998. (Table 4.5)

The number of new cases of breast cancer among senior women has also risen since the early 1980s. As a result, breast cancer remains the leading cause of new cases of cancer among senior women in all age ranges. (Table 4.6)

As with prostate cancer among senior men, growth in the number of newly-diagnosed cases of breast cancer among senior women is greater than increases in deaths from this disease among these women. Part of the reason for the relatively

[3] *Source: National Cancer Institute of Canada, 1996 Canadian Cancer Statistics, Toronto, Canada, 1996.*

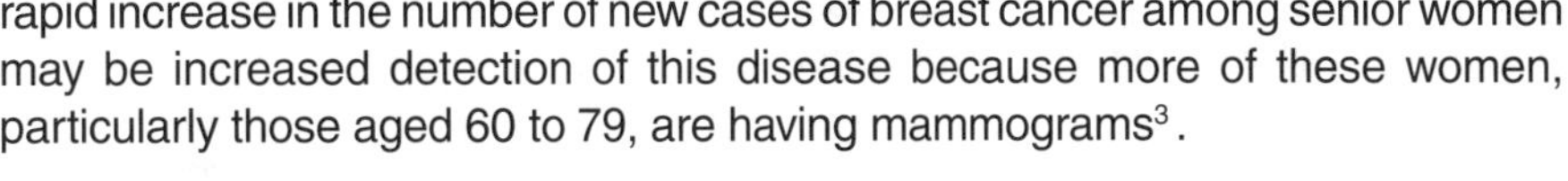

rapid increase in the number of new cases of breast cancer among senior women may be increased detection of this disease because more of these women, particularly those aged 60 to 79, are having mammograms[3].

Suicide rates among seniors

Overall, seniors are somewhat less likely than younger adults to commit suicide. In 1996, there were 14 suicides for every 100,000 people aged 65 and over, compared with 18 per 100,000 population among those aged 25 to 44 and 17 for every 100,000 people aged 45 to 64. (Table 4.7)

As well, the incidence of suicide among seniors has declined since the early 1980s, falling from 18 for every 100,000 seniors in 1981 to 14 per 100,000 population in 1996[4].

Among seniors, men are much more likely than women to commit suicide. In 1996, there were 26 suicides for every 100,000 men aged 65 and over, compared with less than 5 for every 100,000 women in this age range.

In addition, senior men in older age ranges are more likely than their younger counterparts to commit suicide. In 1996, there were 37 suicides for every 100,000 men aged 85 and over, compared with 27 among those aged 75 to 84 and 24 among those aged 65 to 74. In fact, men aged 85 and over were more likely to commit suicide than men in any other age category that year. In contrast, among women, those aged 85 and over were the least likely to commit suicide.

The perceived health of seniors

Most seniors living at home[4] describe their general health in positive terms. In 1996-97, 78% said their health was either good (38%), very good (28%), or excellent (12%), while 16% reported their health was fair and only 6% described it as poor. (Table 4.8)

Among seniors, those in older age groups are the most likely to describe their health as only fair or poor. In 1996-97, 29% of people aged 85 and over and 27% of 75- to 84-year-olds said their health was just fair or poor, compared with 19% of those aged 65 to 74. At all ages, however, seniors living at home describe their health in positive terms. That year, 71% of those aged 85 and over, 73% of those aged 75 to 84, and 81% of those aged 65 to 74, described their health as either good, very good, or excellent.

Women in older age ranges are the most likely to rate their overall health in negative terms. In 1996-97, 30% of women aged 85 and over said their health was either fair or poor. Again, however, the large majority of even women in this group described their health as good, very good, or excellent (70%).

Seniors with chronic health conditions

While most seniors report their overall health is relatively good, many seniors have a chronic health condition as diagnosed by a health professional. In 1996-97,

3 *Source: National Cancer Institute of Canada, 1996 Canadian Cancer Statistics, Toronto, Canada, 1996.*
4 *Source: Statistics Canada, Health Statistics Division.*

82% of all people aged 65 and over living at home reported they had been diagnosed with at least one chronic health condition. (Table 4.9)

Senior women are somewhat more likely than senior men to have a chronic health condition. In 1996-97, 85% of women aged 65 and over had such a problem, compared with 78% of senior men.

Arthritis and rheumatism are the most common chronic health problems reported by seniors. In 1996-97, 42% of people aged 65 and over living at home had been diagnosed by a health professional with one of these problems. At the same time, 33% had high blood pressure, 22% had food or other allergies, 17% had back problems, 16% had chronic heart problems, 15% had cataracts, and 10% had diabetes, while smaller percentages reported having chronic bronchitis or emphysema (6%), asthma (6%), urinary incontinence (6%), sinusitis (5%), ulcers (5%), glaucoma (5%), migraine headaches (4%), or the effects of a stroke (4%).

Activity limitations of seniors

A substantial proportion of seniors reports some level of restriction in their activities because of a long-term health problem. In 1996-97, this was the case for 28% of all people aged 65 and over living in a private household. (Table 4.10)

Among seniors, those in older age ranges are more likely than their younger counterparts to report some level of activity restriction because of a health problem. In 1996-97, 50% of people aged 85 and over were so limited, while the figure was 34% among those aged 75 to 84 and 22% among those aged 65 to 74.

Seniors with disabilities

One in four Canadian seniors has a long-term disability or handicap. In 1996-97, 25% of all people aged 65 and over living at home had such a condition, compared with 20% of people aged 55 to 64 and less than 10% of those between the ages of 25 and 54. (Table 4.11)

Not surprisingly, the proportion of seniors with a long-term disability rises sharply with age. In 1996-97, 45% of those aged 85 and over had a disability or handicap, versus 28% of those aged 75 to 84 and 21% of those aged 65 to 74.

Seniors experiencing chronic pain

A substantial number of seniors also report they suffer from chronic pain or discomfort. In 1996-97, one in four seniors (25%) living at home reported they experienced chronic pain or discomfort, compared with just under 21% of those aged 55 to 64 and only 12% of those between the ages of 25 and 54. (Table 4.12)

Older seniors are more likely than their younger counterparts to experience chronic pain or discomfort. In 1996-97, 37% of people aged 85 and over living at home suffered from chronic pain, compared with 26% of those aged 75 to 84 and 22% of those aged 65 to 74.

For many seniors, chronic pain prevents certain activities. In 1996-97, 20% of the non-institutionalized population aged 65 and over said that chronic pain or

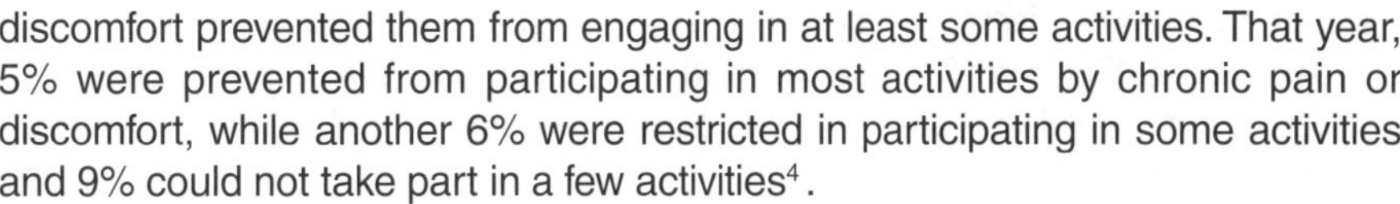

discomfort prevented them from engaging in at least some activities. That year, 5% were prevented from participating in most activities by chronic pain or discomfort, while another 6% were restricted in participating in some activities and 9% could not take part in a few activities[4].

One result of this situation is that many seniors use pain relievers. In 1996-97, 62% of all people aged 65 and over living in a private household used a pain reliever at least once in the month preceding the survey. Seniors, however, are actually no more likely than younger people to take pain killers; indeed, 65% of those between the ages of 25 and 54 had taken a pain reliever in this period. (Table 4.20)

Seniors suffering injuries

Seniors are generally less likely than people in younger age groups to suffer injuries serious enough to limit normal activities. In 1996-97, 6% of all people aged 65 and over suffered such an injury, compared with 8% of 55- to 64-year-olds and 10% of those between the ages of 25 and 54. (Table 4.13)

Senior women are more likely than their male counterparts to suffer an injury. In 1996-97, 7% of women aged 65 and over, versus 4% of senior men, were injured seriously enough to limit normal activities.

Seniors with Alzheimer's disease

A small proportion of seniors had Alzheimer's disease or other dementia. In 1995, 2% of all people aged 65 and over suffered from this condition; that year, an estimated 82,000 seniors had this disease[5].

Most seniors with Alzheimer's or other dementia live in a health-related institution. In 1995, 78% of all those aged 65 and over with this condition were in an institution. That year, 35% of all seniors living in these institutions had Alzheimer's disease or other dementia.

At the same time, only a small percentage of seniors living in a private household had Alzheimer's disease. In 1996-97, just 1% had this condition. As well, most seniors living at home with Alzheimer's are in older age ranges. That year, 5% of all people aged 85 and over living at home had this condition, compared with 1% of those aged 75 to 84 and less than a half a per cent of those aged 65 to 74[4].

Seniors with memory problems

While relatively few seniors have Alzheimer's disease, a substantial proportion reports having some memory problems. In 1996-97, 28% of all people aged 65 and over living in a private household reported they were either somewhat or very forgetful, or could not remember anything at all. (Table 4.14)

The vast majority of these seniors, however, were in the former category; that is, they were somewhat or very forgetful. Indeed, less than a half a per cent could not remember anything at all[4].

[5] *Source: Statistics Canada, National Population Health Survey, 1995.*

Seniors are somewhat more likely than their younger counterparts to have memory problems. In 1996-97, 28% of people aged 65 and over living at home had memory problems, compared with 17% of those aged 55 to 64 and 12% of those between the ages of 25 to 54.

Among seniors, those in older age ranges are the most likely to experience memory problems. In 1996-97, 43% of people aged 85 and over, compared with 32% of those aged 75 to 84 and 23% of 65- to 74-year-olds, were either somewhat or very forgetful, or could not remember anything at all.

Men in older age groups are the most likely to have problems with their memory. In 1996-97, 48% of men aged 85 and over living at home reported these kinds of problems.

Seniors with vision problems

A number of seniors have vision problems that are not corrected by glasses or contact lenses. In 1996-97, 4% of people aged 65 and over living at home could not see well enough to read, even with corrective lenses. This compared with just 1% of those between the ages of 25 and 64. (Table 4.15)

The prevalence of vision problems is highest among seniors in older age groups. In 1996-97, 14% of all people aged 85 and over living at home, compared with 5% of those aged 75 to 84 and 3% of 65- to 74-year-olds, could not see well enough to read, even with corrective lenses.

As well, senior women are more likely than senior men to have vision problems. Among people aged 65 and over living at home, 5% of women, versus 3% of men, could not see well enough to read. Women aged 85 and over, 16% of whom had vision problems, were the most likely seniors to have vision problems.

Seniors with hearing problems

Similarly, a number of seniors have hearing problems. In 1996-97, 4% of people aged 65 and over living at home could not follow a conversation, even with a hearing aid. This compared with just over a half a per cent of those between the ages of 25 and 64. (Table 4.16)

As with vision problems, older seniors are more likely than their younger counterparts to experience hearing problems. In 1996-97, 12% of those aged 85 and over living at home, versus 6% of those aged 75 to 84 and 3% of those aged 65 to 74, could not follow a conversation, even with a hearing aid.

In contrast to seniors with vision problems, senior men were more likely than senior women to have hearing problems in 1996-97: 6% versus 3%. There was little difference, however, in the proportions of senior men and women aged 85 and over with hearing problems.

Seniors consulting with health care professionals

Almost all seniors consult with at least one health care professional over the course of a year. In 1996-97, 96% of all people aged 65 and over living at home reported seeing at least one health care professional. That year, 89% saw a general practitioner, 51% consulted with an eye specialist, 38% went to the dentist or orthodontist, and 29% saw another type of doctor. At the same time, smaller percentages of seniors saw other medical professionals ranging from special care nurses to speech therapists and psychologists. (Table 4.17)

Hospitalization of seniors

Seniors make up a relatively large share of the population that is hospitalized. In 1996-97, there were three times as many hospital separations[6] for every 100,000 people aged 65 and over as there were among people aged 45 to 64. (Table 4.18)

Hospitalization rates are also substantially higher among older seniors than their younger counterparts. In 1996-97, the number of hospital separations for every 100,000 people aged 75 and over was over 70% higher than that among those aged 65 to 74.

Seniors also tend to stay in hospital for considerably longer periods than younger people. In 1996-97, the average hospital visit of people aged 65 and over lasted 17 days, compared with 9 days per visit among those aged 45 to 64, 7 days among people aged 35 to 44, and 6 days or less among those in age groups under age 35.

Older seniors also stay in hospital for longer periods than their younger counterparts. In 1996-97, the average stay per hospital separation among seniors aged 75 and over was 21 days, versus 13 days among those aged 65 to 74.

Senior women tend to stay in hospital longer than senior men. In 1996-97, women aged 65 and over stayed an average of 19 days per hospital visit, compared with 15 days for men in this age range. Most of this difference was accounted for by those in older age ranges. That year, women aged 75 and over stayed in hospital an average of 23 days per visit, compared with 17 days for their male counterparts.

Seniors taking medication

The majority of seniors take some form of prescription or over-the-counter medication. In 1996-97, 84% of all people aged 65 and over living at home took some form of medication in the two days prior to the survey. Indeed, 56% had taken two or more medications in this period. (Table 4.19)

Older seniors are generally more likely than their younger counterparts to take more than one medication. Of seniors living at home in 1996-97, 65% of those aged 85 and over and 61% of those aged 75 to 84, versus 52% of those aged 65 to 74, had taken more than one type of medication in the two days prior to the survey.

---

[6] *Hospital separations refer to the discharge or death of an inpatient. They include individual cases separated, not persons separated, that is, an individual may be counted on more than one occasion.*

Pain relievers are the medication most often taken by seniors. In 1996-97, 62% of those living in a private household had used this type of medication at least once in the month preceding the survey, while 33% had used a medication for blood pressure and 19% had taken another type of heart medication. At the same time, 11% of all seniors took some kind of stomach remedy, 11% used diuretics or water pills, and 10% used a cough or cold medication, while smaller percentages used sleeping pills (8%), thyroid medication (8%), penicillin or other antibiotics (7%), diabetes pills (7%), asthma medication (6%), tranquilizers (5%), anti-depressants (4%), or allergy medicines (3%). As well, 10% of senior women took hormones for menopause or other age-related conditions such as osteoporosis. (Table 4.20)

Seniors who smoke

Seniors are less likely than people in younger age groups to smoke regularly. In 1996-97, 12% of seniors living at home were daily smokers, compared with 21% of those aged 55 to 64 and 28% of those aged 25 to 54. (Table 4.21)

Among seniors, those in younger age ranges are more likely to smoke than their older counterparts. In 1996-97, 15% of people aged 65 to 74 were regular smokers, versus 10% of those aged 75 to 84 and just 2% of people aged 85 and over.

As well, senior men are more likely than senior women to smoke regularly. In 1996-97, 15% of men aged 65 and over living at home smoked on a daily basis, compared with 10% of their female counterparts.

Many seniors, however, are former smokers. In 1996-97, 36% of all seniors, including over half of senior men (52%) and almost one in four senior women (24%), were former smokers.

Alcohol use among seniors

Seniors are also less likely than younger people to use alcohol regularly. In 1996-97, 37% of seniors were regular drinkers, that is, they had at least one drink a month, compared with over 50% of people in age groups under age 65. (Table 4.22)

Younger seniors are more likely than their older counterparts to drink regularly. In 1996-97, 42% of people aged 65 to 74 drank at least once a month, compared with around 30% of those in age groups over age 75.

Senior men are also more likely than senior women to use alcohol regularly. In 1996-97, 49% of senior men, versus 29% of their female counterparts, were regular drinkers.

Seniors are also much less likely than younger people to be heavy drinkers. In 1996-97, just 1% of seniors have five or more drinks on one occasion at least once a week, compared with 4% of people aged 55 to 64 and 5% of those aged 25 to 54. (Chart 4.1)

Chart 4.1

Percentage of people who were heavy drinkers[1], 1996-1997

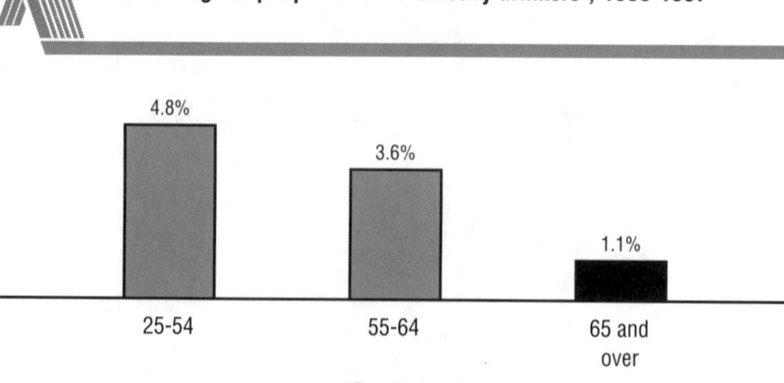

[1] *Includes people who had five or more drinks on one occasion at least once a week in the past twelve months.*

Source: Statistics Canada, National Population Health Survey.

Table 4.1

Life expectancy at birth and at age 65, 1921-1996

	Remaining life expectancy					
	At birth			At age 65		
	Males	Females	Total	Men	Women	Total
	Years					
1921[1,2]	58.8	60.6	59.7	13.0	13.6	13.3
1931[2]	60.0	62.1	61.0	13.0	13.7	13.3
1941[2]	63.0	66.3	64.6	12.8	14.1	13.4
1951	66.4	70.9	68.5	13.3	15.0	14.1
1961	68.4	74.3	71.1	13.6	16.1	14.8
1971	69.4	76.4	72.7	13.8	17.6	15.7
1981	71.9	79.1	75.4	14.6	18.9	16.8
1991	74.6	81.0	77.8	15.8	20.0	18.0
1996[3]	75.7	81.4	78.6	16.3	20.2	18.4

[1] *Excludes Quebec.*
[2] *Excludes Newfoundland.*
[3] *Preliminary estimates.*
Sources: Statistics Canada, Catalogue no. 84-537-XPB; and Health Statistics Division.

Table 4.2

Life expectancy of seniors at selected ages, 1991 and 1996[1]

	Remaining life expectancy					
	Men		Women		Total	
	1991	1996	1991	1996	1991	1996
	Years					
At age:						
65	15.8	16.3	20.0	20.2	18.0	18.4
70	12.6	13.0	16.1	16.3	14.5	14.8
75	9.7	10.1	12.6	12.7	11.4	11.6
80	7.4	7.6	9.5	9.6	8.7	8.8
85	5.5	5.7	7.0	7.0	6.4	6.6
90	4.3	4.4	5.1	5.1	4.8	4.9

[1] *Preliminary estimates.*
Source: Statistics Canada, Health Statistics Division.

Table 4.3

Death rates among people aged 65 and over from selected causes, 1980, 1994 and 1996

	Men			Women			Total		
	1980	1994	1996	1980	1994	1996	1980	1994	1996
	Deaths per 100,000 population[1]								
Cancer	1,414.8	1,543.8	1,544.2	794.9	918.1	888.1	1,054.4	1,177.2	1,150.2
Heart disease	2,520.1	1,726.7	1,720.4	1,654.9	1,160.8	1,080.1	2,022.9	1,404.2	1,343.9
Strokes	612.3	416.8	413.5	550.6	383.0	357.5	578.5	399.6	382.6
Respiratory diseases	624.0	675.6	676.6	251.2	360.7	347.9	400.2	485.0	470.9
Chronic liver disease and cirrhosis	56.5	49.0	48.9	21.8	22.6	19.3	37.1	34.1	32.3
Total all causes	6,369.1	5,597.9	5,632.7	4,108.9	3,806.9	3,618.8	5,055.9	4,559.5	4,429.9

[1] *Figures are age-standardized to the 1991 population.*
Source: Statistics Canada, Health Statistics Division.

Table 4.4

Death rates among men and women aged 65 and over from selected causes, 1980 and 1996

	Seniors aged					
	65-74		75-84		85 and over	
	1980	1996	1980	1996	1980	1996
	Deaths per 100,000 population[1]					
Cancer						
Men	1,074.2	1,090.6	1,919.2	1,963.2	2,585.6	3,107.2
Women	590.2	672.3	968.7	1,095.9	1,485.4	1,601.7
Total	811.0	864.3	1,350.1	1,438.2	1,854.6	2,052.2
Heart Disease						
Men	1,521.0	858.4	3,330.0	2,240.9	7,587.8	5,653.1
Women	702.4	374.6	2,134.6	1,368.4	6,151.4	4,780.1
Total	1,075.8	596.7	2,602.2	1,712.8	6,633.4	5,041.4
Strokes						
Men	257.8	155.3	892.4	565.1	2,272.9	1,606.4
Women	181.4	102.8	740.1	455.0	2,286.4	1,716.7
Total	216.3	126.9	801.3	498.4	2,281.8	1,683.7
Respiratory diseases						
Men	285.2	237.1	845.7	899.6	2,383.4	2,829.9
Women	94.7	127.1	291.7	424.2	1,126.4	1,554.5
Total	181.6	177.6	514.0	611.8	1,548.3	1,936.1
Chronic liver disease and cirrhosis						
Men	69.2	55.6	47.5	31.0	28.4	31.0
Women	25.3	18.5	16.7	14.5	15.2	14.5
Total	45.3	35.5	29.0	19.4	19.6	19.4
Total all causes						
Men	3,789.3	2,936.3	8,511.7	7,237.1	18,958.4	18,019.9
Women	1,933.1	1,615.7	5,186.1	4,478.0	14,427.4	13,982.7
Total	2,779.7	2,221.8	6,520.6	5,566.9	15,947.9	15,190.8

[1] *Figures are age-standardized to the 1991 population.*
Source: Statistics Canada, Health Statistics Division.

Table 4.5

Cancer death rates among people aged 60 and over, by type of cancer, 1980 and 1998[1]

	People aged					
	60-69		70-79		80 and over	
	1980	1998	1980	1998	1980	1998
	Deaths per 100,000 population					
Lung						
Men	290.5	280.3	471.2	518.8	460.8	638.4
Women	67.4	144.2	85.8	222.0	76.8	204.8
Total	172.0	210.2	253.2	350.0	213.4	352.4
Breast						
Women	93.2	80.8	121.8	136.2	168.9	231.5
Prostate						
Men	44.1	55.2	170.5	212.8	510.2	655.7
Colorectal						
Men	85.6	75.3	185.0	153.0	323.7	279.5
Women	62.5	41.2	131.7	84.8	262.3	204.8
Total	73.3	57.7	154.8	114.2	284.2	230.3
Other cancers						
Men	340.6	333.7	636.6	618.5	1,036.4	1,118.1
Women	225.9	228.3	419.4	434.9	773.9	801.4
Total	279.7	279.4	513.8	514.1	867.3	909.3
All cancers						
Men	760.9	744.6	1,463.2	1,503.1	2,331.1	2,691.8
Women	449.0	494.4	758.7	877.8	1,282.0	1,442.6
Total	595.2	615.7	1,064.8	1,147.6	1,655.3	1,867.9

[1] *Figures for 1998 are estimated rates.*

Sources: Statistics Canada, Demography Division; and National Cancer Institute of Canada, Canadian Cancer Statistics, 1998.

Table 4.6

Number of new cases of selected cancers per 100,000 people aged 60 and over, 1980 and 1998[1]

	People aged					
	60-69		70-79		80 and over	
	1980	1998	1980	1998	1980	1998
	New cases per 100,000 population					
Lung						
Men	340.3	350.4	508.9	558.7	421.1	586.7
Women	88.3	197.8	93.4	252.3	76.4	204.8
Total	206.4	271.8	274.0	384.4	199.1	334.8
Breast						
Women	249.8	354.4	271.7	423.8	320.8	409.6
Prostate						
Men	199.8	385.4	548.9	917.8	931.9	1,311.4
Colorectal						
Men	192.4	227.8	341.3	385.8	524.9	534.9
Women	152.3	131.9	258.6	242.2	408.6	374.0
Total	171.1	178.3	294.5	304.1	450.0	428.8
Other cancers						
Men	604.0	621.9	985.8	1,024.2	1,342.1	1,363.2
Women	454.4	461.5	643.4	686.1	847.2	881.6
Total	524.6	543.5	792.2	832.0	1,023.3	1,045.5
All cancers						
Men	1,336.5	1,585.4	2,384.9	2,886.5	3,220.1	3,796.1
Women	944.8	1,145.5	1,267.2	1,604.3	1,653.0	1,870.1
Total	1,128.5	1,363.1	1,752.8	2,157.4	2,210.7	2,525.7

1 *Figures for 1998 are estimated rates.*

Sources: Statistics Canada, Demography Division; and National Cancer Institute of Canada, Canadian Cancer Statistics, 1998.

Table 4.7

Suicide rates, 1996

	Men	Women	Total
		Suicides per 100,000 population	
People aged:			
15-24	23.8	4.6	14.4
25-44	28.4	7.8	18.2
45-64	25.0	8.6	16.8
65-74	24.3	5.4	14.1
75-84	27.4	3.6	13.0
85 and over	36.8	3.3	13.3
Total 65 and over	26.1	4.5	13.7

Source: Statistics Canada, Health Statistics Division.

Table 4.8

General health of people living in a private household, 1996-1997

	Percentage describing their health as					
	Excellent	Very good	Good	Fair	Poor	Total
	%					
People aged:						
25-54						
Men	27.1	41.7	24.7	5.2	1.3	100.0
Women	27.4	39.4	25.2	6.4	1.5	100.0
Total	27.2	40.6	24.9	5.8	1.4	100.0
55-64						
Men	19.9	31.9	31.9	11.7	4.7	100.0
Women	17.8	34.3	31.3	12.1	4.6	100.0
Total	18.8	33.2	31.6	11.9	4.6	100.0
65-74						
Men	13.6	30.0	34.3	16.5	5.7	100.0
Women	13.0	28.3	41.4	13.0	4.2	100.0
Total	13.3	29.0	38.3	14.6	4.8	100.0
75-84						
Men	10.1	24.9	39.5	17.4	8.2	100.0
Women	11.9	25.9	34.7	21.4	6.1	100.0
Total	11.1	25.4	36.7	19.7	7.0	100.0
85 and over						
Men	--	29.1	38.2	16.5	9.9	100.0
Women	6.4	28.5	34.8	19.0	11.3	100.0
Total	6.4	28.8	36.1	18.0	10.8	100.0
Total 65 and over						
Men	12.0	28.4	36.1	16.8	6.7	100.0
Women	12.1	27.5	38.8	16.2	5.4	100.0
Total	12.1	27.9	37.6	16.4	6.0	100.0

Source: Statistics Canada, National Population Health Survey.

Table 4.9

Percentage of seniors living in a private household reporting selected chronic conditions diagnosed by a health professional, 1996-1997

	Seniors aged											
	65-74			75-84			85 and over			Total 65 and over		
	Men	Women	Total	Men	Women	Total	Men	Women	Total	Men	Women	Total
	%											
Food allergies	3.1	8.1	5.9	3.6	7.4	5.8	3.8	4.5	4.2	3.3	7.6	5.7
Other allergies	10.9	22.6	17.4	9.1	19.8	15.3	6.5	9.4	8.3	10.0	20.6	16.0
Asthma	6.0	5.6	5.8	5.2	7.2	6.3	3.2	3.8	3.5	5.6	5.9	5.8
Arthritis/rheumatism	32.2	45.6	39.6	36.0	51.9	45.2	43.1	59.3	53.1	34.1	48.7	42.4
Back problems	15.4	17.6	16.6	12.8	19.7	16.8	20.3	15.8	17.5	14.9	18.1	16.7
High blood pressure	28.2	34.0	31.4	26.0	41.9	35.2	27.4	33.6	31.2	27.4	36.4	32.6
Migraine headaches	2.4	6.2	4.4	--	3.8	2.7	--	--	--	1.9	5.2	3.8
Chronic bronchitis/ emphysema	6.3	4.9	5.5	8.2	7.0	7.5	--	3.0	3.4	6.8	5.4	6.0
Sinusitis	4.0	6.3	5.3	5.1	5.8	5.4	--	3.4	2.7	4.2	5.9	5.1
Diabetes	11.2	8.8	9.9	13.6	9.7	11.3	--	7.4	11.9	12.4	9.0	10.4
Heart disease	15.7	11.3	13.3	22.4	18.4	20.1	20.1	22.8	21.8	18.1	14.4	16.0
Ulcers	5.6	3.3	4.3	6.3	4.1	5.0	1.7	6.6	4.7	5.5	3.8	4.6
Cataracts	6.6	10.9	9.0	19.4	25.6	23.0	28.6	32.9	31.3	12.0	17.3	15.0
Cancer	5.3	4.2	4.7	6.4	4.9	5.6	10.8	3.9	6.5	6.0	4.4	5.1
Effects of a stroke	3.5	2.1	2.7	7.3	3.8	5.3	7.7	8.2	8.0	5.0	3.1	3.9
Urinary incontinence	2.9	5.1	4.1	7.2	8.4	7.9	5.3	13.4	10.3	4.4	6.8	5.8
Glaucoma	3.6	3.7	3.7	6.2	7.0	6.7	3.9	8.7	6.9	4.4	5.2	4.9
Any long-term condition	76.4	82.4	79.7	81.6	88.9	85.8	76.8	88.1	83.8	78.0	84.9	81.9

Source: Statistics Canada, National Population Health Survey.

Table 4.10

Percentage of people living in a private household limited in at least some activities because of a chronic health condition, 1996-1997

	Men	Women	Total
		%	
People aged:			
25-54	9.5	11.7	10.9
55-64	20.7	20.7	20.7
65-74	22.8	20.9	21.7
75-84	33.8	34.8	34.4
85 and over	42.4	53.9	49.5
Total 65 and over	27.4	28.0	27.8

Source: Statistics Canada, National Population Health Survey.

Table 4.11

Percentage of people living in a private household with long-term disabilities or handicaps, 1996-1997

	Men	Women	Total
		%	
People aged:			
25-54	8.6	9.6	9.1
55-64	19.7	19.4	19.6
65-74	22.2	19.7	20.8
75-84	28.9	27.0	27.8
85 and over	46.0	44.4	45.0
Total 65 and over	25.8	24.0	24.8

Source: Statistics Canada, National Population Health Survey.

Table 4.12

Percentage of people living in a private household experiencing chronic pain or discomfort, 1996-1997

	Men	Women	Total
		%	
People aged:			
25-54	11.0	12.4	11.7
55-64	18.1	22.9	20.6
65-74	19.9	23.9	22.1
75-84	25.1	27.1	26.2
85 and over	37.4	37.2	37.3
Total 65 and over	22.6	26.0	24.6

Source: Statistics Canada, National Population Health Survey.

Table 4.13

Percentage of people living in a private household injured[1] in the past 12 months, 1996-1997

	Men	Women	Total
		%	
People aged:			
25-54	11.8	8.3	10.1
55-64	6.5	10.0	8.3
65-74	3.7	5.8	4.9
75-84	5.2	8.0	6.8
85 and over	5.9	9.7	8.3
Total 65 and over	4.3	6.8	5.7

[1] *Refers to injuries that were serious enough to limit normal activities.*
Source: Statistics Canada, National Population Health Survey.

Table 4.14

Percentage of people living in a private household with memory problems, 1996-1997

	Men	Women	Total
		%	
People aged:			
25-54	11.3	13.6	12.4
55-64	16.3	18.3	17.3
65-74	23.4	23.0	23.2
75-84	36.2	29.4	32.4
85 and over	48.1	40.3	43.2
Total 65 and over	29.0	26.5	27.6

Source: Statistics Canada, National Population Health Survey.

Table 4.15

Percentage of people living in a private household with vision[1] problems, 1996-1997

	Men	Women	Total
		%	
People aged:			
15-64	1.0	1.0	1.0
65-74	1.9	3.1	2.6
75-84	3.7	6.7	5.4
85 and over	10.4	16.0	13.9
Total 65 and over	3.1	5.3	4.4

1 Refers to those who cannot see well enough to read, even with corrective lenses.
Source: Statistics Canada, National Population Health Survey.

Table 4.16

Percentage of people living in a private household with hearing[1] problems, 1996-1997

	Men	Women	Total
		%	
People aged:			
25-64	0.7	0.6	0.6
65-74	3.4	1.8	2.5
75-84	9.1	3.9	6.1
85 and over	10.7	12.4	11.7
Total 65 and over	5.7	3.3	4.3

[1] *Refers to those who cannot hear a normal conversation, even with a hearing aid.*
Source: Statistics Canada, National Population Health Survey.

Table 4.17

Percentage of people living in a private household consulting with a health care professional in the past 12 months, 1996-1997

	Family doctor/ general practi- tioner	Eye specialist	Other medical doctor	Dentist/ ortho- dontist	Nurse	Chiro- practor	Physio- therapist	Social worker/ counselor	Psycho- logist	Speech therapist	Total consulting with any health profes- sional
						%					
People aged:											
25-54	75.8	31.6	23.3	61.8	5.1	11.9	7.0	3.3	3.0	1.0	91.8
55-64	83.6	38.8	28.0	49.2	5.1	10.9	7.7	1.8	1.2	0.8	93.1
65-74	87.0	47.8	29.4	41.3	6.0	7.9	5.1	1.6	0.4	1.3	94.6
75-84	91.4	55.7	30.0	33.9	8.7	7.4	6.5	1.7	0.3	1.9	96.9
85 and over	91.8	54.9	26.6	28.4	15.9	8.9	10.1	4.0	0.1	4.0	96.9
Total 65 and over	88.7	50.8	29.4	38.1	7.6	7.8	5.9	1.8	0.4	1.7	95.5

Source: Statistics Canada, National Population Health Survey.

Table 4.18

Hospital separations and average days per separation in general and allied special hospitals, 1996-1997

	Separations[1] per 100,000 population			Average days per visit		
	Males	Females	Total	Males	Females	Total
People aged:						
Under 1	25,562	18,838	22,284	5.4	5.6	5.5
1-4	6,809	5,199	6,055	3.0	3.4	3.2
5-14	2,940	2,605	2,777	4.4	4.4	4.4
15-19	3,456	7,607	5,473	6.0	4.2	4.8
20-24	3,525	13,364	8,352	7.2	3.5	4.3
25-34	3,974	16,814	10,321	7.0	3.8	4.4
35-44	5,112	8,803	6,956	7.3	6.0	6.5
45-64	10,593	9,883	10,235	8.6	9.2	8.9
65-74	26,869	20,296	23,318	12.1	13.8	12.9
75 and over	46,661	36,248	40,132	17.1	23.1	20.5
Total 65 and over	34,173	27,562	30,361	14.6	19.4	17.1

1 *Hospital separations refer to the discharge or death of an inpatient. They include individual cases separated, not persons separated, that is, an individual may be counted on more than one occasion.*
Source: Canadian Institute for Health Information, Hospital Morbidity Database.

Table 4.19

Percentage of people living in a private household taking medications in the two days before the survey, by the number of medications[1], 1996-1997

	Percentage taking		
	One medication	Two or more	Total taking at least one medication
		%	
People aged:			
25-54	29.4	17.3	46.7
55-64	30.7	39.8	70.6
65-74	30.4	52.4	82.8
75-84	26.2	61.4	87.6
85 and over	20.4	64.6	85.0
Total 65 and over	28.3	56.2	84.4

1 *Includes both prescription and over-the-counter medications.*
Source: Statistics Canada, National Population Health Survey.

Table 4.20

Percentage of people living in a private household taking selected medications in the month before the survey, 1996-1997

	People aged					
	25-54	55-64	65-74	75-84	85 and over	Total 65 and over
	%					
Pain relievers	65.2	61.9	60.5	63.8	64.9	61.9
Tranquilizers	2.4	4.3	5.0	4.8	5.4	4.9
Anti-depressants	3.9	4.0	3.9	4.8	--	4.4
Sleeping pills	2.7	4.3	6.2	10.7	9.6	7.9
Blood pressure medication	4.0	20.4	31.1	35.3	33.1	32.6
Other heart medication	1.4	7.5	14.7	24.8	27.8	18.8
Cough or cold remedies	17.4	12.1	10.1	9.0	7.3	9.5
Penicillin/other antibiotics	8.4	7.4	7.0	6.4	4.3	6.6
Asthma medication	4.0	5.4	5.6	6.1	3.7	5.6
Allergy medicines	7.9	5.4	3.8	2.4	1.4	3.2
Pills to control diabetes	0.8	4.1	7.0	7.1	10.8	7.3
Stomach remedies	8.3	10.9	10.4	12.6	9.3	11.0
Thyroid medication	3.2	6.6	7.6	8.8	6.1	7.9
Hormones for menopause or aging symptoms[1]	7.2	26.3	13.1	6.1	0.7	9.9
Diuretics or water pills	1.5	5.4	10.1	12.3	13.9	11.0

[1] *Includes women only.*
Source: Statistics Canada, National Population Health Survey.

Table 4.21

Smoking status of people living in a private household, 1996-1997

	Daily smokers	Occasional smokers	Former daily smokers [1]	Never smoked
			%	
People aged:				
25-54				
Men	30.6	4.2	24.4	36.6
Women	25.6	3.5	22.7	43.6
Total	28.1	3.9	23.6	40.1
55-64				
Men	23.4	2.7	44.2	26.3
Women	19.4	2.0	25.6	48.9
Total	21.3	2.3	34.5	38.1
65-74				
Men	17.4	2.4	50.8	25.1
Women	12.6	2.3	26.4	54.7
Total	14.7	2.4	37.3	41.6
75-84				
Men	13.1	--	54.4	26.6
Women	7.7	3.6	23.1	58.7
Total	10.0	2.8	36.4	45.1
85 and over				
Men	--	--	54.6	25.4
Women	--	--	14.1	77.9
Total	2.4	--	29.6	57.8
Total 65 and over				
Men	15.1	2.4	52.2	25.6
Women	10.2	2.4	24.4	57.9
Total	12.3	2.4	36.4	43.9

[1] Includes people who smoke occasionally.
Source: Statistics Canada, National Population Health Survey.

Table 4.22

Percentage of people living in a private household who used alcohol, by frequency, 1996-1997

	Regular drinkers[1]	Occasional drinkers[2]	Abstainers
		%	
People aged:			
25-54			
Men	72.0	13.0	4.8
Women	49.1	27.5	9.3
Total	60.6	20.2	7.0
55-64			
Men	63.0	14.8	7.0
Women	40.4	26.1	13.2
Total	51.2	20.7	10.2
65-74			
Men	53.4	17.5	7.2
Women	33.3	23.4	17.9
Total	42.2	20.8	13.1
75-84			
Men	39.7	22.4	9.3
Women	23.4	22.1	23.9
Total	30.3	22.2	17.7
85 and over			
Men	42.7	17.7	11.9
Women	19.6	16.3	36.2
Total	28.4	16.8	26.9
Total 65 and over			
Men	48.5	19.0	8.2
Women	29.1	22.4	21.3
Total	37.4	21.0	15.6

1 Refers to people who take a drink at least once a month.
2 Refers to people who take a drink less than once a month.
Source: Statistics Canada, National Population Health Survey.

Education and Literacy

Educational attainment of seniors

Seniors have relatively low levels of formal educational training. As of 1996, for example, only 8% of all Canadians aged 65 and over had a university degree, compared with 13% of those aged 55 to 64 and over 20% of those between the ages of 25 and 54. (Table 5.1)

In fact, the majority of today's seniors, over six out of ten, never completed high school. Of these, 25% had attended, but had not graduated from high school, while 37% had less than a Grade 9 education.

It should be pointed out, however, that the educational opportunities and facilities that were available to today's seniors when they were young were considerably more limited than they were for subsequent generations. As such, the educational attainment levels of seniors will be greater in the future than they are today, just as today's seniors are actually better educated than seniors were in the past.

Educational differences by age and gender

Senior men are somewhat more likely than senior women to be university graduates. In 1996, 11% of men aged 65 and over, versus 6% of their female counterparts, were university graduates. (Table 5.2)

The difference between the proportions of senior men and women with university degrees, however, will likely decline in the future as this gap is smaller among men and women in age groups under age 65; indeed, women make up the majority of all university students in Canada today.

The formal educational attainment of seniors is also lower among those in older age groups than among younger seniors. In 1996, for example, 6% of seniors aged 85 and over had a university degree, compared with 7% of those aged 75 to 84 and 9% of 65- to 74-year-olds. At the same time, almost half (48%) of all those aged 85 and over had less than a Grade 9 education, compared with 39% of those aged 75 to 84 and 34% of those aged 65 to 74. Again, however, these differences reflect, to a large degree, variation in educational opportunities available to succeeding generations.

Going back to class

While seniors have relatively low levels of formal educational experience, a substantial number are currently enrolled in some type of adult education program. In 1997, just over 175,000 Canadians aged 65 and over, 5% of the total senior population, were enrolled in some kind of educational program[1] .

[1] *Source: Statistics Canada, 1998 Adult Education and Training Survey.*

The largest number of seniors participating in education or training programs in 1997, just under 100,000, or 3% of all seniors, were involved in non-academic courses, workshops, seminars, or tutorials. A similar number of seniors, about 85,000, were taking hobby, recreational, or personal interest courses, while a small number of seniors, about 6,000 in total, were taking courses leading to a degree, certificate, or diploma.

Low literacy levels

Partly as a result of their relative lack of formal educational experience, many seniors have difficulty reading. In 1994, over half of all Canadians aged 66 and over performed at the lowest level on the prose scale in the International Adult Literacy Survey. That year, 53% were able to perform only simple reading tasks, such as locating one piece of information in a text. (Chart 5.1)

Computer usage among seniors

A growing number of seniors have computers in their homes. In 1997, 13% of households headed by someone aged 65 and over owned a computer, up from 5% in 1990. (Chart 5.2)

The proportion of senior households with a computer, though, is still well below that of households with head under age 65. In 1997, 13% of senior households owned a computer, compared with 42% of household headed by someone under age 65.

Senior family households are generally more likely to have a computer than seniors who live alone. In 1997, 18% of family households headed by someone aged 65 and over had a computer, compared with just 7% of seniors who lived by themselves. As well, among seniors who live alone, men were twice as likely as women to own a computer: 10% versus 5%[2].

Seniors are also less likely than younger people to use computer communications services, such as the Internet. In 1997, just 6% of households with head aged 65 and over reported computer communications usage at any location, including home, work, or school; this compared with almost 40% of households with head aged either 35 to 54 or under 35, and 21% of those with head aged 55 to 64. (Chart 5.3)

[2] Source: Statistics Canada, Catalogue no. 11-010-XPB, February 1999.

Chart 5.1

Percentage of the population at the lowest literacy level, 1994

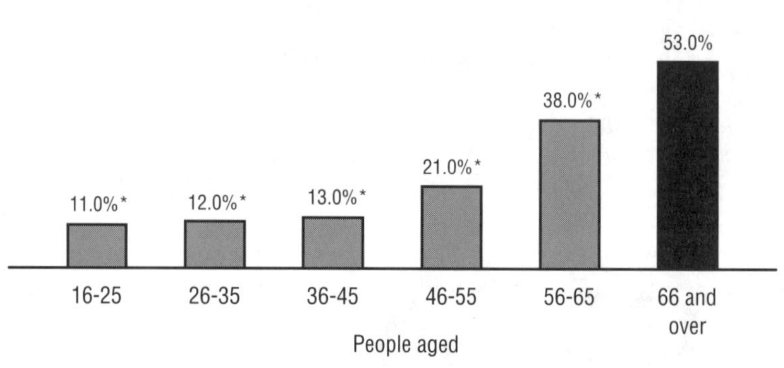

** Figure should be used with caution because of the small size of the sample.*
Source: Statistics Canada, International Adult Literacy Survey.

Chart 5.2

Percentage of households with computers, 1990-1997

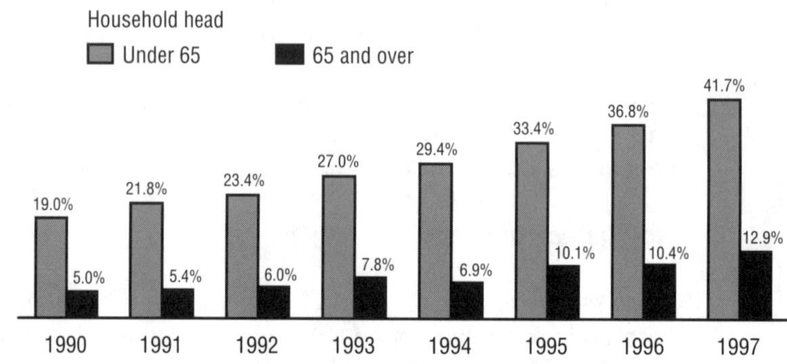

Source: Statistics Canada, Catalogue no. 13-218-XPB.

Chart 5.3

Percentage of households using computer communications, by age of household head, 1997

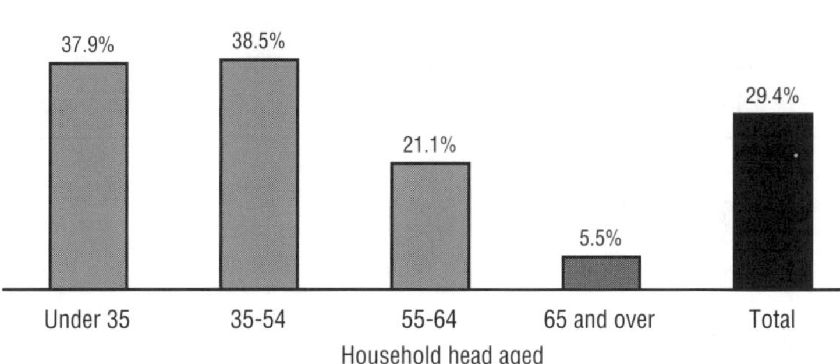

Source: Statistics Canada, Catalogue no. 11-010-XPB.

The relatively low rate of computer communications use by seniors reflects, at least in part, the fact that senior households are much less likely than other households to be connected to the Internet. In 1997, only 4% of households headed by someone aged 65 and over had Internet service, compared with 15% of households with head under age 65. The proportion of senior households with an Internet connection that year, however, was double what it was just a year earlier, when the figure was only 2%[3].

[3] *Source: Statistics Canada, Household Facilities and Equipment Survey, 1997.*

Table 5.1

Educational attainment, 1996

	People aged			
	25-44	45-54	55-64	65 and over
	%			
Less than Grade 9	4.1	11.1	24.4	36.8
Some secondary	16.6	17.5	22.7	24.7
High school graduate	19.3	20.0	17.4	14.4
Non-university postsecondary	31.0	24.9	19.1	13.4
University without degree	8.3	6.1	3.6	2.6
University graduate	20.7	20.4	12.8	8.1
Total	100.0	100.0	100.0	100.0

Source: Statistics Canada, 1996 Census of Canada.

Table 5.2

Educational attainment of seniors, 1996

	Less than Grade 9	Some secondary	High school graduate	Non-university postsecondary	University without degree	University graduate	Total
				%			
Seniors aged:							
65-74							
Men	34.5	22.0	15.0	13.8	3.2	11.4	100.0
Women	34.2	26.9	15.0	14.9	2.5	6.5	100.0
Total	34.4	24.6	15.0	14.4	2.8	8.8	100.0
75-84							
Men	39.8	22.8	14.1	11.1	2.7	9.6	100.0
Women	39.0	27.1	13.9	12.3	2.2	5.6	100.0
Total	39.3	25.4	14.0	11.8	2.4	7.2	100.0
85 and over							
Men	49.4	19.4	11.4	9.2	2.3	8.3	100.0
Women	47.0	22.7	10.9	12.6	1.9	4.9	100.0
Total	47.8	21.7	11.0	11.4	2.0	6.1	100.0
65 and over							
Men	36.9	22.1	14.6	12.8	3.0	10.7	100.0
Women	36.8	26.6	14.3	13.9	2.4	6.1	100.0
Total	36.8	24.7	14.4	13.4	2.6	8.1	100.0

Source: Statistics Canada, 1996 Census of Canada.

Paid Work and Volunteer Participation

Few seniors employed

While the majority of Canadians seniors are retired[1], a substantial number are still part of the paid workforce. In 1998, just over 225,000 people aged 65 and over, 6% of the total senior population, had jobs. (Table 6.1)

The proportion of seniors currently with jobs, though, is lower than it was in the mid-1970s, when around 9% were part of the paid workforce. Most of this decline, however, occurred in the 1970s and 1980s. In fact, there has been little change in the proportion of seniors in the paid workforce since the early 1990s.

Among seniors, men are considerably more likely than women to be working outside the home. In 1998, 10% of men aged 65 and over were part of the paid workforce, compared with 3% of senior women. The share of senior men with jobs, though, is down sharply from 1976, when 16% were employed. In contrast, there was only a small change, from 4% to 3%, in the proportion of senior women participating in the paid workforce in this period.

Decline in employment among men aged 55 to 64

One of the most dramatic labour force trends in Canada in the last several decades has been the decline in the workforce participation of men aged 55 to 64. Between 1976 and 1995, the proportion of these men with jobs fell from 74% to 54%. The employment level of men in this age range, though, has rebounded somewhat since 1995, rising to 56% in 1998. (Table 6.1)

In contrast to men aged 55 to 64, the share of women in this age range participating in the paid workforce has increased since the mid-1970s. In 1998, 36% of these women were employed outside the home, up from 30% in 1976. Women in this age range, however, are still considerably less likely than their male counterparts to be employed outside the home.

Many senior women never part of paid workforce

A substantial proportion of senior women have never been part of the paid workforce. In 1998, 22% of all women aged 65 and over, compared with just 2% of men in this age range, had never worked outside the home. (Chart 6.1)

[1] *Source: Statistics Canada, Catalogue no. 89-546-XPE.*

Chart 6.1

Percentage of the population never employed, 1998

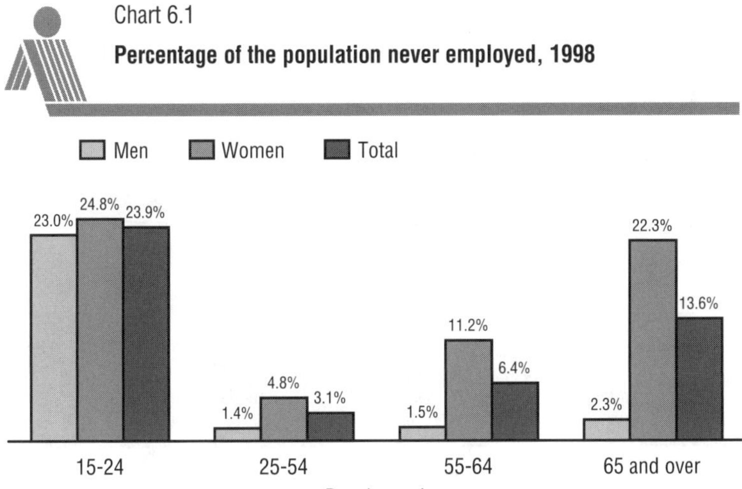

Source: Statistics Canada, Labour Force Survey.

Chart 6.2

Percentage employed part time, 1998

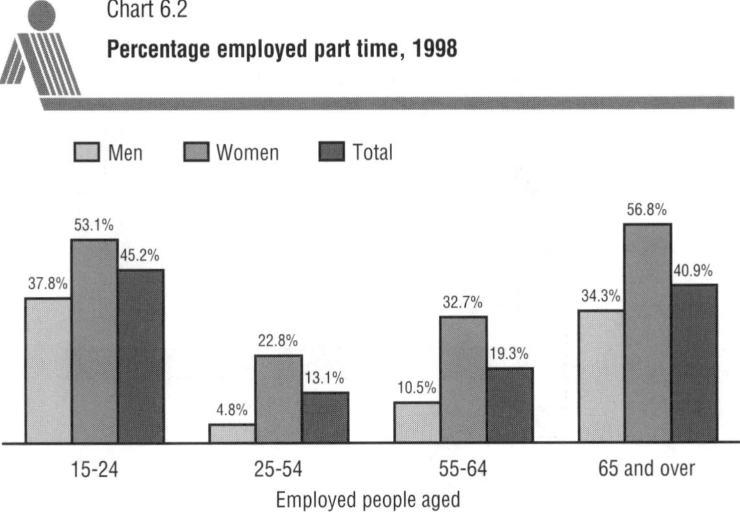

Source: Statistics Canada, Labour Force Survey.

This situation will change in the future, however, because women in younger age groups are currently much more likely to be part of the paid workforce than were their senior counterparts. Indeed, by 1998, only 11% of women aged 55 to 64, and just 5% of those aged 25 to 54, had never been employed outside the home.

Part-time work

Many employed seniors work part-time. In 1998, 41% of all people aged 65 and over who participated in the paid workforce were employed on a part-time basis. In contrast, this was the case for only 19% of workers aged 55 to 64 and just 13% of those between the ages of 25 and 54. On the other hand, employed 15- to 24-year-olds, among whom the figure was 45%, were slightly more likely than seniors to work part-time that year. (Chart 6.2)

As in other age groups, employed senior women are more likely than their male counterparts to be employed part-time. In 1998, 57% of women aged 65 and over who participated in the paid workforce worked part-time, compared with 34% of employed senior men.

Many self-employed or unpaid family workers

Almost two out of three employed seniors are either self-employed or unpaid family workers. In 1998, 63% of all those aged 65 and over who participated in the paid workforce were in one of these categories. This was over twice the figure for employed people aged 55 to 64, only 29% of whom were self-employed or unpaid family workers that year; it was also almost three times the figure for those aged 45 to 54 (22%) and four times that for 25- to 44-year-olds (16%). (Chart 6.3)

Senior men are more likely than senior women to be either self-employed or unpaid family workers. In 1998, 67% of employed men aged 65 and over, versus 53% of their female counterparts, were in one of these categories.

Occupational distribution of employed seniors

A relatively large share of employed seniors work in agriculture. In 1998, 19% of all people aged 65 and over who participated in the paid workforce worked in agriculture, compared with only 3% of the labour force aged 15 to 64. (Table 6.2)

As a result, seniors represent a substantial share of the agricultural workforce in Canada. In 1998, 10% of all agriculture workers were aged 65 and over, whereas seniors made up only 2% of the overall workforce. (Chart 6.4)

Seniors make up an even greater share of those employed in religious professions. In 1998, 14% of all people employed in these professions were aged 65 and over. Seniors also made up 2% of both the sales and transportation workforces in Canada, while they represented 1% or less of those employed in all other occupational groups.

As with younger workers, there are differences in the occupational distributions of employed senior men and women. Senior men were considerably more likely than their female counterparts to work in agriculture, manufacturing, construction, and transportation in 1998; they were also more likely to have managerial jobs. In contrast, senior women were more likely to work in clerical, sales, or service occupations. That year, 55% of all women aged 65 and over with jobs, versus 27% of employed senior men, worked in one of these areas. (Table 6.2)

Unemployment among seniors

A small number of seniors are officially unemployed, that is, they are out of work, but are looking for a job. In 1998, just 3% of labour force participants aged 65 and over were unemployed, compared with around 7% for both those aged 25 to 54 and 55 to 64 and 15% for 15- to 24-year-olds. (Chart 6.5)

Formal volunteer activities

While relatively few seniors are still in the paid workforce, many more stay active in their communities through participation in formal volunteer activities. In 1997, more than 800,000 Canadians aged 65 and over, 23% of the total senior population, participated in these kinds of activities. (Chart 6.6)

Seniors, though, are somewhat less likely than people in younger age ranges to participate in formal volunteer activities. In 1997, 23% of seniors were involved in such activities, compared with 30% of people aged 55 to 64 and 33% of those between the ages of 25 and 54. (Chart 6.6)

Chart 6.3

Percentage of workers who were self-employed or unpaid family workers, 1998

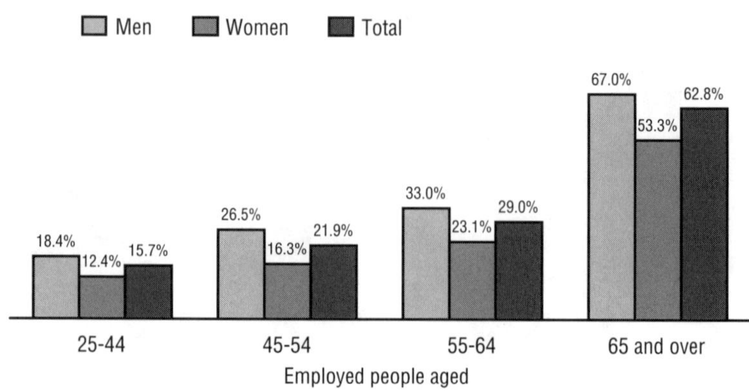

Source: Statistics Canada, Labour Force Survey.

Chart 6.4

Seniors as a percentage of total employed in selected occupations, 1998

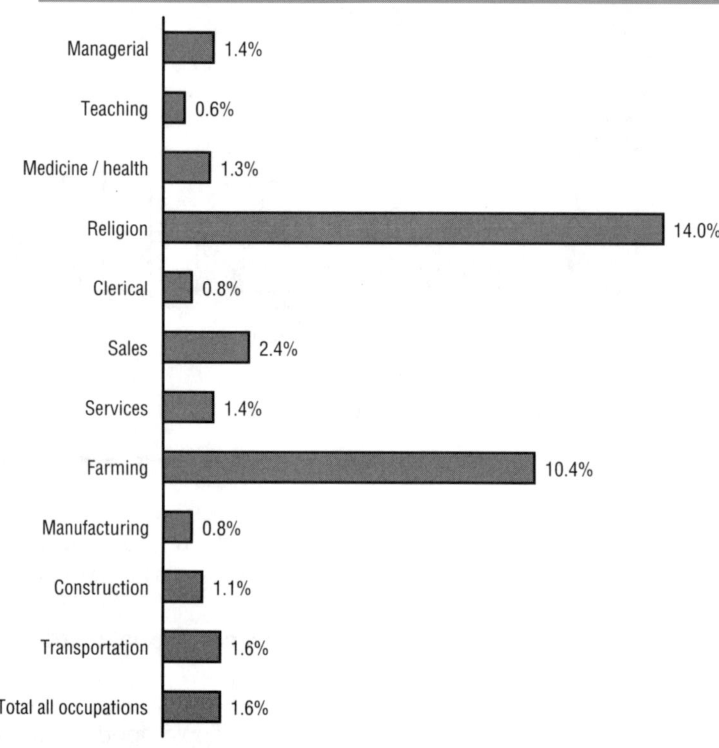

Source: Statistics Canada, Labour Force Survey.

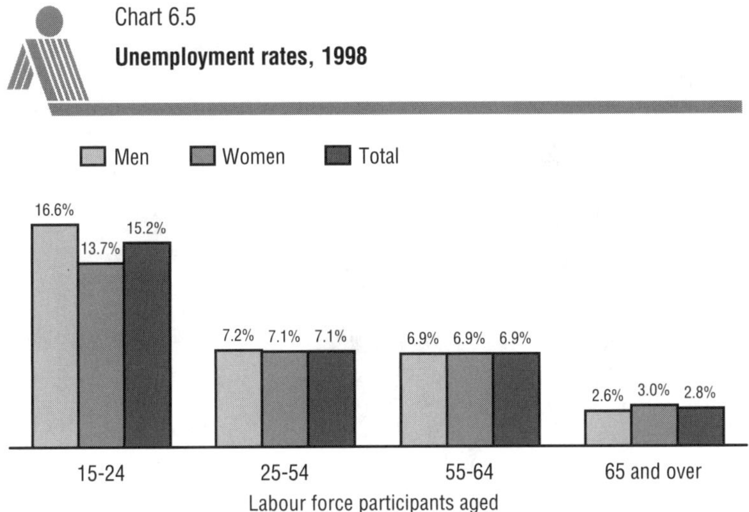

Source: Statistics Canada, Labour Force Survey.

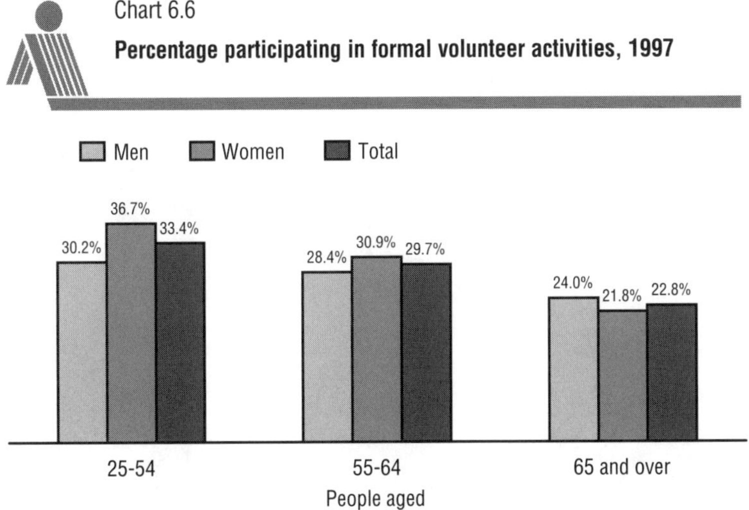

Source: Statistics Canada, National Survey on Giving, Volunteering and Participating.

Seniors are somewhat less likely than younger adults to participate in formal volunteer activities, in part, because many seniors, especially those in older age groups, are prevented from doing so by health limitations. Indeed, almost two out of three seniors that did not engage in formal volunteer work in 1997 reported it was because they were physically unable to participate[2].

However, while a smaller percentage of seniors than other adults engage in volunteer activities, those seniors that do participate spend considerably more time on these activities than younger people. In 1997, senior volunteers averaged 3.9 hours per week on these activities, compared with 3.1 hours for volunteers aged 45 to 64 and 2.7 hours for those aged 25 to 44[2].

Senior volunteers are active in a wide range of volunteer activities including participation as unpaid board or committee members; organizing and supervising group activities; canvassing and fundraising; providing care and support to others through an agency; collecting, serving, and delivering food; doing executive and administrative work; and engaging in public education and lobbying activities[2].

Informal volunteer activity

Even greater numbers of seniors participate in informal volunteer activities outside their homes. In 1997, 58% of all seniors participated in such endeavours. (Chart 6.7)

As with formal volunteer work, seniors participate in a wide range of informal volunteer activities including visiting other seniors; providing babysitting services; helping with shopping and transportation; providing care and support to the sick; helping out with housework; writing letters and helping fill out forms; and helping with gardening, household maintenance, and snow shovelling[2].

Among seniors, men and women are about as likely to engage in informal volunteer activities. There are differences, though, in the types of these activities engaged in by senior women and men. Senior women, for example, are more likely to help others with housework, do babysitting, visit with other seniors, and provide care and support for the sick. Senior men, on the other hand, are more likely to help with gardening, household maintenance, snow shovelling, shopping, and transportation, as well as writing letters and filling out forms[2].

[2] Source: Statistics Canada, 1997 National Survey on Giving, Volunteering and Participating.

Charitable donations

Many seniors also contribute to volunteer activities by making financial donations. In 1997, 80% of all seniors made at least one such contribution. This was about the same as figures in younger age groups; seniors, however, made larger contributions, on average, than people in other age groups. That year, seniors donated an average of $328 to charities, compared with $313 among those aged 55 to 64, $291 among those aged 45 to 54, $260 for 35- to 44-year-olds, and $160 among those aged 25 to 34[2].

Chart 6.7

Percentage participating in informal help outside household, 1997

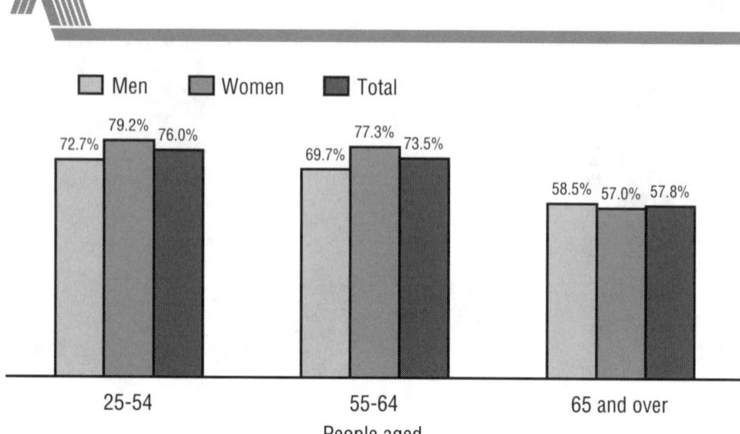

Source: Statistics Canada, National Survey on Giving, Volunteering and Participating.

Table 6.1

Percentage employed, 1976-1998

	People aged											
	15-24			25-54			55-64			65 and over		
	Men	Women	Total	Men	Women	Total	Men	Women	Total	Men	Women	Total
	%											
1976	59.4	50.6	55.0	90.4	48.7	69.7	73.6	30.3	51.3	15.7	4.1	9.3
1977	59.1	50.3	54.7	89.7	50.1	70.0	72.5	30.4	50.7	15.3	4.3	9.2
1978	59.7	51.5	55.6	89.8	52.4	71.3	72.3	30.9	50.7	15.0	4.5	9.1
1979	62.3	54.0	58.2	90.4	54.2	72.4	72.9	32.3	51.7	15.1	4.2	9.0
1980	62.5	55.4	59.0	90.0	56.4	73.3	72.8	32.0	51.5	14.6	4.3	8.8
1981	62.6	56.2	59.5	90.0	58.7	74.4	71.9	32.3	51.2	13.9	4.4	8.5
1982	55.3	53.0	54.2	85.8	58.1	72.0	68.5	31.6	49.2	13.6	4.2	8.3
1983	54.3	52.9	53.6	84.6	59.1	71.9	66.4	30.9	47.9	12.8	3.9	7.8
1984	56.8	54.0	55.4	84.7	60.4	72.6	65.5	30.9	47.5	12.5	4.2	7.8
1985	57.8	56.1	57.0	85.7	62.2	74.0	64.4	31.2	47.2	12.1	4.2	7.6
1986	60.2	57.5	58.9	86.5	64.2	75.4	63.6	31.0	46.7	11.5	3.6	7.0
1987	61.8	58.7	60.3	87.2	65.8	76.5	62.1	32.5	46.8	11.6	3.4	6.9
1988	63.5	59.9	61.7	87.9	67.9	78.0	62.4	33.3	47.4	11.2	3.7	6.9
1989	64.4	61.0	62.7	88.0	69.1	78.6	62.0	32.3	46.8	10.8	4.0	6.9
1990	61.5	59.4	60.4	86.6	70.0	78.4	60.9	33.5	47.0	11.2	3.7	6.9
1991	56.1	56.8	56.5	83.8	69.2	76.4	57.3	32.8	44.8	10.9	3.3	6.6
1992	53.4	54.0	53.7	81.8	68.4	75.2	56.0	33.2	44.4	10.4	3.3	6.4
1993	52.3	52.3	52.3	82.2	68.6	75.4	55.0	33.0	43.9	9.6	3.5	6.1
1994	53.2	51.9	52.5	82.7	68.9	75.8	54.6	34.3	44.3	10.5	3.3	6.4
1995	53.1	51.9	52.5	83.2	69.6	76.4	54.0	33.4	43.6	9.8	3.2	6.0
1996	52.4	50.8	51.6	83.1	69.9	76.5	54.7	34.1	44.2	9.9	3.3	6.2
1997	52.2	49.7	51.0	83.9	70.5	77.2	56.1	33.6	44.7	9.9	3.4	6.2
1998	53.0	52.1	52.6	84.7	71.8	78.3	55.5	35.6	45.4	10.3	3.3	6.4

Source: Statistics Canada, Labour Force Survey.

Table 6.2

Occupational distribution, 1998

	Workers aged					
	15-64			65 and over		
	Men	Women	Total	Men	Women	Total
	%					
Managerial	13.9	14.2	14.1	13.0	10.1	12.2
Professional						
Teaching	2.9	6.8	4.7	1.0	4.7	1.7
Medicine	1.9	9.4	5.3	4.2	4.9	4.4
Religion	0.3	0.1	0.2	2.8	0.9	2.3
Other professional	10.8	7.6	9.3	9.7	8.2	8.9
Total professional	15.9	23.9	19.6	17.1	17.8	17.3
Clerical	5.3	27.9	13.8	2.0	19.9	7.3
Sales	9.7	10.3	10.0	14.4	17.7	15.3
Service	10.5	17.3	13.6	10.3	17.2	12.3
Primary						
Farming	3.9	1.9	3.0	21.9	12.3	19.0
Other primary	1.8	0.1	1.0	--	--	--
Total primary	5.7	2.0	4.0	24.2	12.9	20.8
Manufacturing	18.8	5.5	12.7	8.2	2.8	6.6
Construction	9.1	0.4	5.1	5.0	--	3.6
Transportation	6.2	0.8	3.7	4.9	--	3.8
Other	4.8	1.7	3.4	1.9	--	1.5
Total	100.0	100.0	100.0	100.0	100.0	100.0
Total employed (000s)	7,643.8	6,456.4	14,100.2	158.8	67.4	226.2

Source: Statistics Canada, Labour Force Survey.

Income and Expenditures

Average income of seniors rising

The incomes of seniors have risen faster than those of people under the age of 65 since the early 1980s. In fact, the average income of people aged 65 and over in 1997 was 18% higher than it was in 1981, once the effects of inflation have been accounted for, whereas the figure among people aged 15 to 64 actually declined in the same period. (Chart 7.1)

Seniors, however, still have lower incomes, on average, than people in most age groups under age 65. In 1997, people aged 65 and over had an average income from all sources of just over $20,000, compared with $34,200 among those aged 45 to 54, $32,300 among those aged 35 to 44, $27,300 among people aged 55 to 64, and $26,700 among those aged 25 to 34. Seniors, though, did have considerably greater incomes than 15- to 24-year-olds, who averaged just over $10,000 that year. (Table 7.1)

As in other age groups, men aged 65 and over have higher incomes than their female counterparts. In 1997, senior men had an average income of $26,150, slightly more than $10,000 more than their female counterparts, among whom the figure was only $16,100.

The incomes of both senior women and men, however, have risen since the early 1980s. The average annual income of men aged 65 and over in 1997 was 19% higher than in 1981, once the effects of inflation had been accounted for, while the figure for senior women was up 17% in the same period. (Chart 7.2)

Incomes of elderly families

There was a similar pattern among families. In 1997, families headed by someone aged 65 and over had an average income of $43,351, a figure which was considerably lower than those for all two-spouse families headed by non-seniors, but higher than those of families

Chart 7.1

Average real income, 1981 and 1997

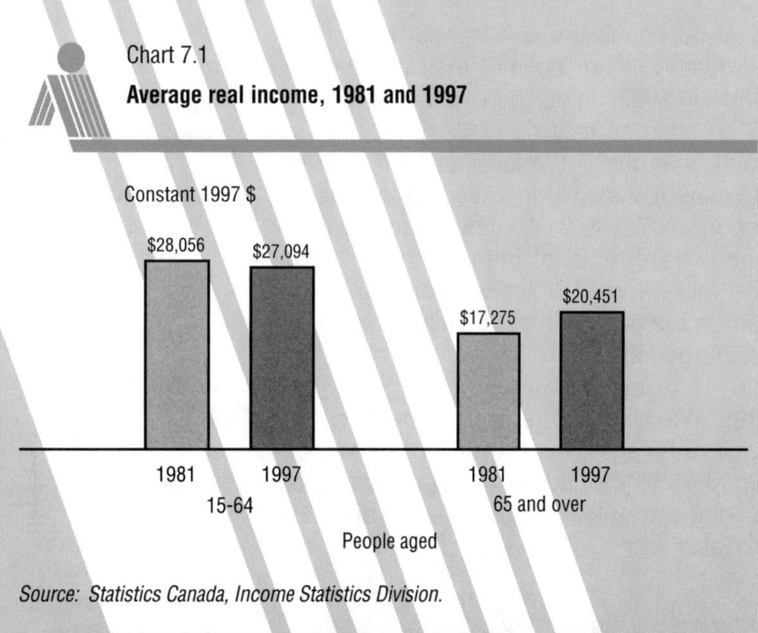

Source: Statistics Canada, Income Statistics Division.

headed by either a male or female lone-parent under the age of 65. (Chart 7.3)

The real incomes of senior families, though, have generally risen faster than those of other families since the early 1980s. The average income of families with head aged 65 and over was 10% higher in 1997 than in 1980, once increases in the cost of living have been accounted for, whereas figures among families headed by someone under age 65 varied from a 5% increase for these families with children to a 3% decline among male-headed lone-parent families.

Among seniors who live with their spouse, men have considerably higher incomes than women. In 1997, married men aged 65 and over had an average income of $26,950, almost twice the figure for married women in this age range ($13,760). (Chart 7.4)

Incomes of unattached seniors

Unattached seniors[1] also have lower average incomes than unattached individuals in most younger age ranges. In 1997, unattached individuals aged 65 and over had an average income of $19,950, whereas the figures among their counterparts between the ages of 25 and 64 ranged from over $31,000 for those aged 35 to 54 to $20,500 for those aged 60 to 64. Unattached seniors, however, had higher incomes than unattached individuals aged 15 to 24, who averaged $16,500 per person that year. (Table 7.2)

As in the overall population, unattached senior men have considerably higher incomes than their female counterparts. In 1997, unattached men aged 65 and over had an average income of $24,300, almost $6,000 more than the figure for unattached senior women ($18,400). As well, the average income of these men in 1997 was 24% higher than it was in 1980, once the effects of inflation have been accounted for, whereas there was only an 17% increase in the average incomes of unattached senior women in this period. (Chart 7.5)

The average income of unattached seniors declines somewhat in older age groups. In 1997, unattached people aged 65 to 69 had an average income of $21,400, compared with $19,500 for those aged 70 and over. (Table 7.2)

[1] An unattached individual is a person who either lives alone or in a household where he/she is not related to other household members.

Chart 7.2

Average income of individuals, 1981 and 1997

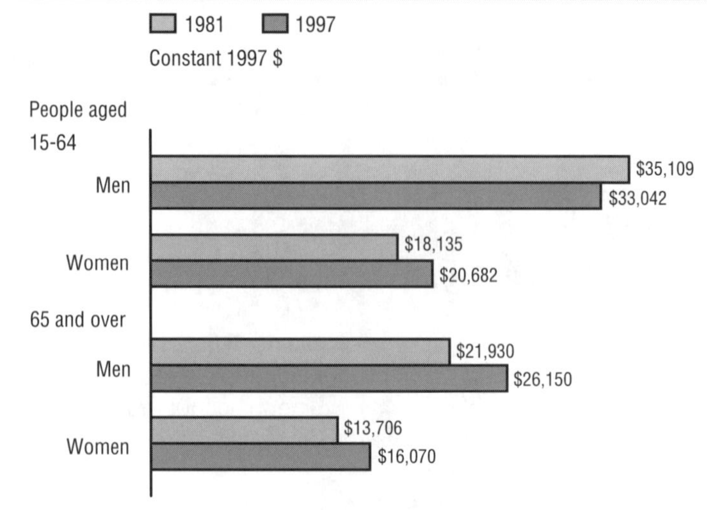

Source: Statistics Canada, Catalogue no. 13-207-XPB.

Chart 7.3

Average real income of families, 1980 and 1997

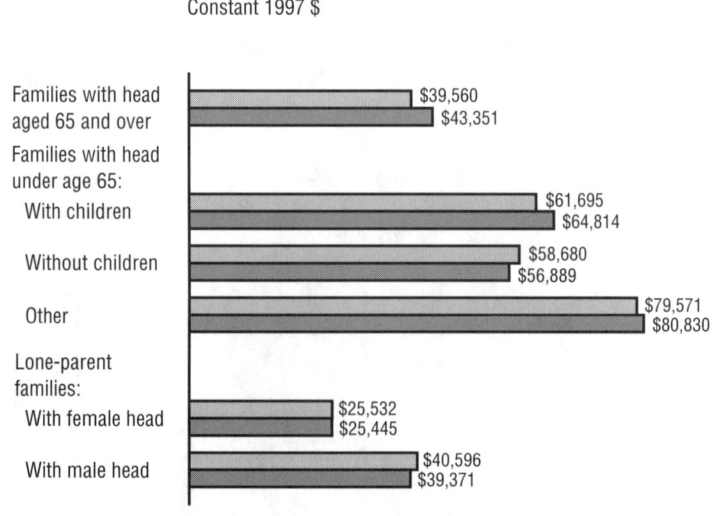

Sources: Statistics Canada, Catalogue no. 13-207-XPB; and Income Statistics Division.

Chart 7.4

Average income of people aged 55 and over, by marital status, 1997

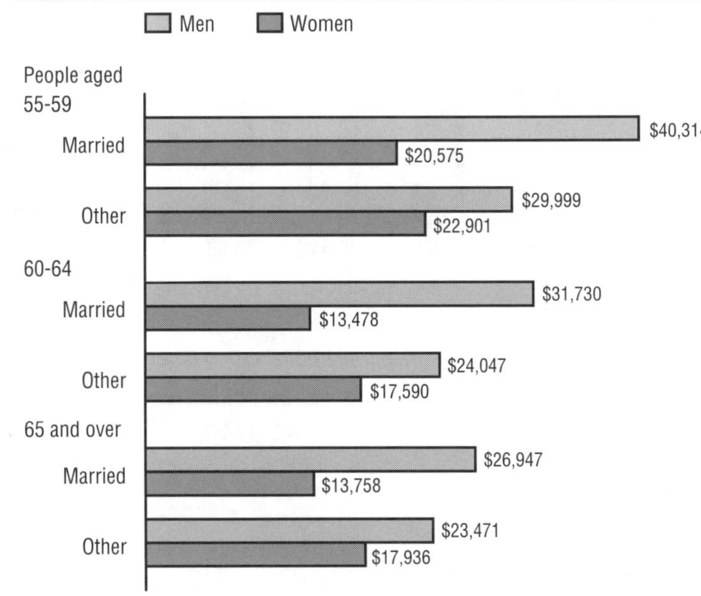

Source: Statistics Canada, Income Statistics Division.

Chart 7.5

Average real income of unattached seniors, 1980 and 1997

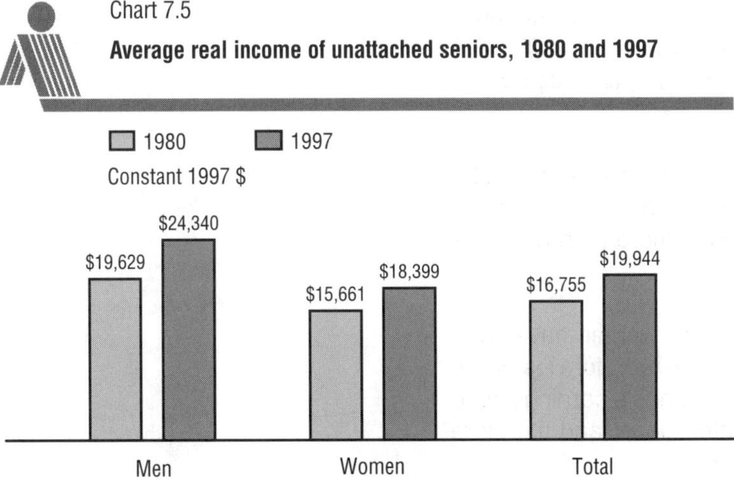

Source: Statistics Canada, Catalogue no. 13-207-XPB.

Income of seniors in the provinces

Seniors in Ontario and the western provinces have higher incomes, on average, than those in Quebec and the Atlantic provinces. In 1997, seniors in both Ontario and British Columbia had an average income of over $22,000, while the figures were close to $22,000 in Alberta and almost $20,000 in Manitoba and Saskatchewan. In contrast, seniors in Quebec had an average income of $17,900 that year, while in the Atlantic provinces the figure ranged from almost $18,000 in New Brunswick to less than $15,000 in Newfoundland. (Table 7.3)

There was a corresponding pattern in the incomes of families headed by seniors. In 1997, the average income of families with head aged 65 and over ranged from a high of almost $48,500 in Ontario to $29,800 in Newfoundland. Similarly, the figure among unattached seniors ranged from $21,100 in Ontario to $15,900 in Newfoundland.

Sources of seniors' income

The largest share of the income of seniors comes from the Old Age Security (OAS) program. In 1997, 29% of all the income of seniors came from this program, while 21% came from private retirement pensions, 21% came in the form of Canada and Quebec Pension Plan (C/QPP) benefits, 12% came from investments other than Registered Retirement Savings Plans (RRSPs), 8% was income from employment, and 5% was income from RRSPs. (Table 7.4)

Most of the gains in the overall average incomes of seniors, however, have come from work-related pensions. Between 1981 and 1997, for example, the share of the income of seniors coming from C/QPP doubled from 10% to 21%. In fact, total C/QPP benefits, averaged over all seniors, were almost $2,700 greater in 1997 than in 1981, once the effects of inflation were factored in.

Similarly, the share of the income of seniors coming from private employment pensions almost doubled between 1981 and 1997, rising from 12% to 21%. In that period, there was a $2,100 per person increase in pay-outs from these pension plans, when averaged over all seniors.

On the other hand, there has been little change in average Old Age Security payments received by seniors in the past decade and a half. Indeed, the average income received by people aged 65 and over from this program in 1997 was a few dollars less per person than in 1981, once the effects of inflation have been accounted for. As a result, the share of the income of seniors coming from OAS fell from 34% to 29% in this period.

At the same time, there have been major declines in the income of seniors coming from both investments and employment sources. In 1997, seniors received an average of $2,280 less per person from investment sources other than RRSPs than was the case in 1981, while there was an average decline of $550 per senior in income from employment. As a result, the share of all income of seniors coming from investment sources other than RRSPs fell from 27% in 1981 to 12% in 1997, while the share accounted for by employment income dropped from 12% to 8% in the same period.

Chart 7.6

Percentage of taxfilers making RRSP contributions, 1997

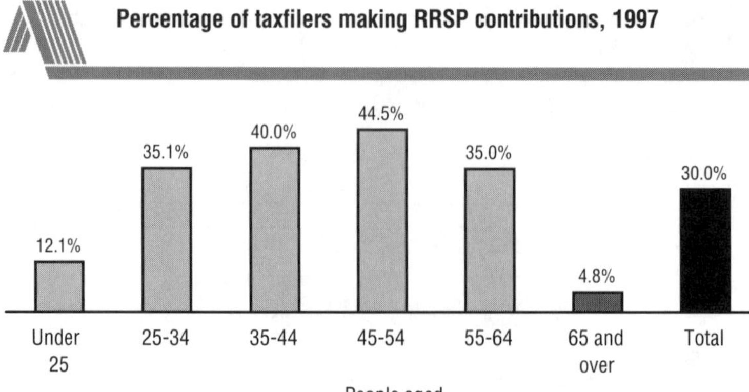

Source: Statistics Canada, Small Area and Administrative Data Division.

Some of the decline in investment income received by seniors, however, has been offset by income from RRSPs. In 1997, people aged 65 and over received an average of about $900, or 5% of their total income, from these plans.

As well, the share of the income of seniors derived from RRSPs may increase in the future because a growing number of Canadians are contributing to RRSPs. In 1997, 30% of all tax filers contributed to an RRSP, including 45% of those aged 45 to 54, 40% of those aged 35 to 44, and 35% of both those aged 25 to 34 and 55 to 64. (Chart 7.6)

Different seniors, different income sources

There is also considerable variation in the impact of the various income sources on the incomes of senior men and women. Old Age Security benefits, for example, make up a particularly large share of the incomes of senior women. In 1997, 38% of all income of women aged 65 and over came from this program, compared with 21% of that of their male counterparts. (Table 7.5)

In contrast, private employment-related retirement pensions provide a greater share of the income of senior men than that of senior women. In 1997, 27% of the income of men aged 65 and over came from these plans, more than twice the figure for senior women (13%).

This difference results, in part, from the fact that historically women have been less likely than men to be part of the paid work force and were therefore less likely to contribute to a private pension plan. As well, because women's earnings were lower than those of their male counterparts, their contributions, and therefore their subsequent benefits, were, in many cases also lower.

Chart 7.7

Percentage of paid workers covered by a Registered Pension Plan, 1989-1997

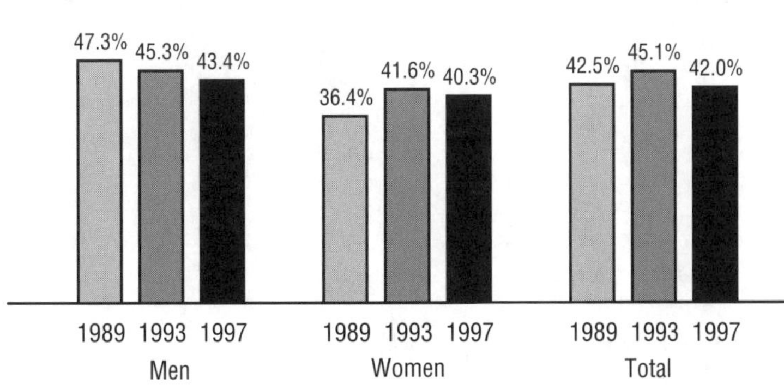

Source: Statistics Canada, Catalogue no. 74-401-SPB.

The difference between the proportions of the income of senior men and women coming from private retirement pensions, however, is likely to narrow in the future. On the one hand, the proportion of women who are working continues to rise, while that of men is falling. In addition, the share of working women covered by these plans has grown in the last decade, while that of men has fallen. In 1997, 40% of employed women were part of a Registered Pension Plan, up from 36% in 1989. In contrast, the share of employed men covered by these plans fell from 47% to 43% in the same period. (Chart 7.7)

In contrast to private retirement pensions, Canada/Quebec Pension Plan benefits account for about the same share of the incomes of senior men and women. In 1997, 21% of all income of men aged 65 and over and 22% of that of women in this age range came from this source.

In terms of actual dollars, however, senior men received, on average, over $2,000 more per year in C/QPP benefits in 1997 than senior women. Again, this difference reflects, in part, the fact that in the past women were less likely than their male counterparts to be employed, and were therefore less likely to contribute to this program. As well, even when these women were employed, their earnings were lower than those of men and as such, their C/QPP contributions were also lower. As a result, their subsequent benefits are also lower. In addition, survivor benefits, which are received mostly by women, are only 60% the retirement pension the deceased spouse would have received.

There are also differences in the distribution of the sources of income of seniors depending on their family status. Private employment-related retirement pensions, as well as income from employment, provide much greater shares of the income of families headed by seniors than that of unattached seniors, whereas Old Age Security and Canada and Quebec Pension Plan benefits provide greater shares of the income of unattached seniors. For example, in 1997, OAS benefits made up 33% of the income of unattached seniors, compared with 21% of that of families headed by people aged 65 and over. Similarly, C/QPP benefits represented 23% of the income of unattached seniors, versus 18% of that of families headed by seniors. (Table 7.6)

Similarly, among unattached seniors, private retirement pensions and income from employment contribute larger shares of the income of men than that of their female counterparts, while unattached senior women receive a much greater share of their income from the Old Age Security program. In 1997, 37% of all income of unattached women aged 65 and over were OAS benefits, compared with 25% of that of unattached senior men.

Government income security programs for seniors

The primary government transfer programs aimed at seniors are the Old Age Security (OAS) program and the Canada/Quebec Pension Plans (C/QPP). OAS benefits are available to all Canadian citizens or legal residents aged 65 and over who have resided in Canada for a sufficient period. Seniors with little or no income other than OAS may also be eligible for additional benefits in the form of a Guaranteed Income Supplement (GIS).

C/QPP benefits are available as early as age 60 to those who contributed to these plans. These plans cover all employees and self-employed people in Canada, except those with very small earnings; for those covered, contributions are compulsory. As well, survivors of deceased contributors to these programs are entitled to benefits.

Low income among seniors

Less than one in five seniors in Canada lives in a low-income situation. In 1997, almost two thirds of a million people aged 65 and over, 19% of all seniors, had incomes below Statistics Canada's Low Income Cut-offs[2]. (Table 7.7)

The proportion of seniors with low incomes, however, has fallen sharply over the past 17 years, dropping from 34% in 1980 to 19% in 1997. In contrast, the incidence of low income has risen among both adults between the ages of 18 and 64 and children under age 18 in this period. As a result, seniors were less likely than children under age 18 to live in a low-income situation in 1997, while they were still somewhat more likely than adults under age 64 to have low incomes. Both situations, however, contrast sharply with those in the early 1980s, when seniors were more than twice as likely as both children and other adults to live in a low-income situation.

Among seniors, women are more than twice as likely as men to have low incomes. In 1997, 24% of all women aged 65 and over lived in a low-income situation, compared with 12% of their male counterparts.

There is also wide variation in the proportion of seniors with low incomes in different provinces. In 1997, the share of seniors with low incomes ranged from 28% in Quebec to 13% in Saskatchewan and Nova Scotia. In the remaining provinces, the figure was 15% in Prince Edward Island and New Brunswick, 14% in Ontario and Alberta, 20% in British Columbia, and 19% in Newfoundland. (Table 7.8)

[2] *Families or individuals are classified as having low income if they spend, on average, at least 20 percentage points more of their pre-tax income than the Canadian average on food, shelter, and clothing. Using 1992 as the base year, families and individuals with incomes below the Low Income Cut-offs usually spend more than 54.7% of their income on these items and are considered to be in straitened circumstances. The number of people in the family and the size of the urban or rural area where the family resides are also taken into consideration. Note, however, that Statistics Canada's Low Income Cut-offs are not official poverty lines. They have no officially recognized status as such, nor does Statistics Canada promote their use as poverty lines.*

Low income and family status among seniors

There is also considerable variation in the incidence of low income among seniors depending on their family status; in particular, unattached seniors are far more likely than those that live in families to have low incomes. In 1997, 45% of all unattached individuals aged 65 and over were considered to have low incomes, compared with only 6% of seniors that lived with either their spouse or other immediate family members. (Table 7.9)

As well, among unattached seniors, women are considerably more likely than their male counterparts to have low incomes. In 1997, almost half of these women (49%) lived in a low-income situation, compared with 33% of their male counterparts.

In contrast, there is almost no difference in the proportions of senior women and men living in a family with low income. In 1997, 6% of men and 5 % of women were classified as living in a low-income situation.

The incidence of low income among both unattached senior women and men, however, has dropped sharply since the early 1980s. Between 1980 and 1997, the share of these women with low incomes fell from 72% to 49%, while among men the figure fell from 61% to 33%.

There has also been a substantial drop in the percentage of seniors living in families with low incomes. In 1997, around 6% of both women and men aged 65 and over who were part of a family lived in a low-income situation, compared with 18% for both in 1980.

In fact, families headed by seniors currently have lower rates of low income than other families. In 1997, 7% of families headed by people aged 65 and over had low incomes, compared with 15% of all two-spouse families with head under age 65, 24% of lone-parent families headed by men, and 56% of female-headed lone-parent families. (Table 7.10)

Expenditures of seniors

As with the rest of the population, seniors devote a large share of their overall spending to basics such as food, shelter, clothing, and transportation. In 1997, senior family households[3] spent 49% of their total budgets on these items, about the same figure as non-senior family households (48%). That year, 17% of all senior family household expenditures went to shelter costs, while 13% was spent on food, 14% went to transportation costs, and 4% to clothing. (Table 7.11)

Seniors who live alone devote an even greater share of their budgets to these basic items. In 1997, 53% of their expenditures, versus 47% of those of their non-senior counterparts, went to food, shelter, transportation, and clothing.

Shelter costs account for a particularly large share of all expenditures of seniors who live alone. In 1997, over one in four (26%) dollars spent by these people went to cover shelter costs.

---

[3] *Senior family households are those in which the individual primarily responsible for the financial maintenance of the household is aged 65 and over.*

Gifts and contributions also account for a relatively large share of the overall spending of seniors. In 1997, gifts and contributions represented 6% of the total spending of senior family households and 9% of that of unattached individuals aged 65 and over. These figures were both three times higher than those of their non-senior counterparts.

Seniors pay less in taxes than younger people. In 1997, personal taxes accounted for 18% of the total expenditures of senior family households and 13% of that of seniors who lived alone. In contrast, taxes accounted for 22% of the total expenditures of both other family households and individuals under age 65 who lived alone.

Table 7.1

Average income, 1997

	Men	Women	Total
		$	
People aged:			
15-24	11,558	9,220	10,411
25-34	31,487	21,692	26,692
35-44	39,641	24,626	32,343
45-54	42,199	25,321	34,213
55-64	34,852	18,244	27,269
65 and over	26,150	16,070	20,451
Total	32,104	19,847	26,042

Source: Statistics Canada, Income Statistics Division.

Table 7.2

Average income of unattached individuals, 1997

	Men	Women	Total
		$	
People aged:			
15-24	17,681	15,248	16,501
25-34	29,059	26,152	28,009
35-44	32,422	30,675	31,871
45-54	32,472	29,764	31,313
55-59	29,748	21,708	25,611
60-64	23,078	18,944	20,497
65-69	25,802	18,987	21,367
70 and over	23,698	18,252	19,526
Total 65 and over	24,340	18,399	19,944
Total	28,106	21,945	25,005

Source: Statistics Canada, Income Statistics Division.

Table 7.3

Average income of seniors, by family status and province, 1997

	All seniors			Unattached seniors			Families with head aged 65 and over
	Men	Women	Total	Men	Women	Total	
				$			
Newfoundland	17,385	12,223	14,562	15,237	16,190	15,906	29,767
Prince Edward Island	22,629	13,977	17,756	16,769	16,747	16,752	37,669
Nova Scotia	21,615	14,465	17,471	20,363	18,194	18,714	34,818
New Brunswick	22,423	14,604	17,958	15,858	17,355	17,005	37,117
Quebec	23,122	14,117	17,887	21,301	16,157	17,479	38,434
Ontario	28,359	17,243	22,104	26,944	19,180	21,132	47,484
Manitoba	25,818	15,533	19,944	24,133	17,384	19,234	41,967
Saskatchewan	25,354	15,414	19,809	21,654	17,669	18,765	40,413
Alberta	27,088	17,298	21,685	25,320	19,147	20,909	45,590
British Columbia	27,961	17,382	22,150	27,030	21,249	22,811	46,071
Canada	26,150	16,070	20,451	24,340	18,399	19,944	43,351

Source: Statistics Canada, Income Statistics Division.

Table 7.4

Income of seniors, by source, 1981, 1994 and 1997

	1981[1]		1994[1]		1997	
	$	%	$	%	$	%
Wages and salaries	1,625	9.4	989	4.9	991	4.8
Net income from self-employment	477	2.8	421	2.1	558	2.7
Total employment income	2,100	12.1	1,410	7.0	1,549	7.6
Investment income						
Interest/bonds	3,758	21.7	1,890	9.4	1,511	7.4
Dividends	482	2.8	441	2.2	470	2.3
Other	407	2.4	402	2.0	385	1.9
Total investment income	4,646	26.9	2,733	13.6	2,366	11.6
RRSPs[2]	--	--	760	3.8	949	4.6
Income from government transfers						
Old Age Security[3]	5,876	34.0	6,065	30.2	5,873	28.7
C/QPP	1,679	9.7	4,118	20.4	4,376	21.4
Unemployment insurance	37	0.2	66	0.3	26	0.1
Social assistance	236	1.4	201	1.0	150	0.7
Other government transfers	271	1.6	545	2.7	628	3.1
Total government transfers	8,098	46.8	10,995	54.7	11,054	54.1
Retirement pensions[2]	2,123	12.3	3,846	19.1	4,211	20.6
Other money income	307	1.8	360	1.8	322	1.6
Total	17,275	100.0	20,103	100.0	20,451	100.0

[1] *Expressed in 1997 dollars.*
[2] *Data on income from RRSPs were included with retirement pensions in 1981.*
[3] *Includes Guaranteed Income Supplements.*
Source: Statistics Canada, Income Statistics Division.

Table 7.5

Sources of income of individuals, 1997

	People aged					
	15-64			65 and over		
	Men	Women	Total	Men	Women	Total
	%					
Wages and salaries	80.7	78.8	80.0	6.5	2.8	4.8
Net income from self-employment	8.5	5.2	7.3	4.1	1.0	2.7
Total employment income	89.2	84.0	87.3	10.6	3.8	7.6
Investment income						
Interest/bonds	0.8	1.3	1.0	6.1	9.0	7.4
Dividends	0.6	0.5	0.5	2.6	1.9	2.3
Other	0.6	0.5	0.5	2.0	1.8	1.9
Total investment income	2.0	2.2	2.1	10.7	12.7	11.6
RRSPs	0.1	0.1	0.1	4.7	4.5	4.6
Income from government transfers						
Old Age Security[1]	0.0	0.2	0.1	21.2	38.1	28.7
C/QPP	0.9	1.3	1.0	21.1	21.8	21.4
Unemployment insurance	1.7	1.9	1.8	0.2	0.1	0.1
Social assistance	1.3	2.5	1.7	0.5	1.0	0.7
Other government transfers	1.5	4.3	2.5	3.0	3.1	3.1
Total government transfers	5.4	10.2	7.2	46.0	64.2	54.1
Retirement pensions	2.2	1.6	2.0	26.5	13.2	20.6
Other money income	1.1	1.9	1.4	1.5	1.7	1.6
Total	100.0	100.0	100.0	100.0	100.0	100.0
Total income ($)	33,042	20,682	27,094	26,150	16,070	20,451

1 Includes Guaranteed Income Supplements.
Source: Statistics Canada, Income Statistics Division.

Table 7.6

Sources of income of seniors, by family status, 1997

	Families with head aged 65 and over	Unattached seniors		
		Men	Women	Total
		%		
Wages and salaries	18.1	4.4	1.3	2.3
Net income from self-employment	3.8	3.8	0.6	1.6
Total employment income	21.8	8.2	1.9	3.9
Investment income				
Interest/bonds	6.4	6.7	8.6	8.0
Dividends	2.7	0.7	1.3	1.1
Other	1.8	1.4	1.9	1.7
Total investment income	10.9	8.9	11.8	10.8
RRSPs	4.2	3.8	4.6	4.3
Income from government transfers				
Old Age Security[1]	21.2	25.2	37.2	33.4
C/QPP	17.6	21.3	23.4	22.7
Unemployment insurance	0.6	0.2	--	0.1
Social assistance	0.9	0.8	1.1	1.0
Other government transfers	2.4	3.6	4.1	4.0
Total government transfers	42.8	51.1	65.8	61.2
Retirement pensions	19.1	25.3	14.6	18.0
Other money income	1.2	2.7	1.3	1.7
Total	100.0	100.0	100.0	100.0
Total income ($)	43,351	24,340	18,399	19,944

[1] *Includes Guaranteed Income Supplements.*

Source: Statistics Canada, Income Statistics Division.

Table 7.7

Percentage of the population with low income, 1980-1997[1]

	1980	1982	1984	1986	1988	1990	1992	1994	1996	1997
					%					
People aged:										
Under 18										
Males	15.5	18.6	21.0	17.7	15.7	17.3	19.1	18.9	20.9	20.6
Females	16.1	19.6	21.0	17.5	16.5	18.2	19.3	20.1	21.4	19.0
Total	15.8	19.1	21.0	17.6	16.1	17.8	19.2	19.5	21.1	19.8
18-64										
Men	11.6	13.5	14.6	13.0	11.6	11.8	14.1	14.2	14.6	15.1
Women	15.5	16.1	18.1	16.1	15.2	15.2	17.0	17.5	17.8	17.8
Total	13.6	14.8	16.4	14.6	13.4	13.5	15.5	15.9	16.2	16.4
65 and over										
Men	26.6	20.0	22.0	19.3	16.6	13.7	12.7	10.7	12.8	11.7
Women	39.8	36.0	35.1	32.0	32.7	27.1	26.8	25.8	27.0	24.0
Total	34.0	29.1	29.5	26.6	25.8	21.3	20.8	19.3	20.8	18.7

1 Based on Statistics Canada's Low Income Cut-offs, 1992 base.
Source: Statistics Canada, Catalogue no. 13-207-XPB.

Table 7.8

Percentage of seniors with low income, by province, 1997[1]

	Men	Women	Total
		%	
Newfoundland	14.0	23.2	19.0
Prince Edward Island	10.5	17.9	14.7
Nova Scotia	9.0	16.2	13.2
New Brunswick	8.0	19.8	14.7
Quebec	18.6	34.7	27.9
Ontario	8.3	18.6	14.1
Manitoba	13.3	29.7	22.6
Saskatchewan	5.6	19.6	13.4
Alberta	8.3	17.9	13.6
British Columbia	12.6	25.2	19.5
Canada	11.7	24.0	18.7

1 Based on Statistics Canada's Low Income Cut-offs, 1992 base.
Source: Statistics Canada, Income Statistics Division.

Table 7.9

Percentage of seniors with low income, by family status, 1980-1997[1]

	In families			Unattached individuals		
	Men	Women	Total	Men	Women	Total
	%					
1980	18.0	17.5	17.8	60.7	71.6	68.6
1981	18.6	16.8	17.8	57.3	70.0	66.6
1982	13.4	13.3	13.3	52.3	70.4	65.9
1983	14.7	12.5	13.7	57.0	71.3	67.8
1984	15.6	14.5	15.0	54.6	65.7	63.1
1985	14.2	13.1	13.6	50.2	64.1	60.9
1986	13.4	11.8	12.6	48.4	61.2	58.1
1987	12.4	10.7	11.5	41.9	59.3	55.1
1988	11.9	10.9	11.4	38.9	61.4	56.1
1989	9.4	8.4	8.9	35.5	56.6	51.5
1990	7.4	6.6	7.0	41.0	53.8	50.7
1991	7.8	8.2	8.0	40.7	54.2	50.9
1992	7.9	8.2	8.1	34.9	54.0	49.2
1993	8.9	8.4	8.7	39.0	56.4	51.9
1994	5.9	6.3	6.1	31.8	52.9	47.6
1995	7.0	6.7	6.9	28.7	50.6	45.1
1996	7.5	7.8	7.6	33.3	53.4	47.9
1997	6.4	5.4	5.9	33.3	49.1	45.0

[1] *Based on Statistics Canada's Low Income Cut-offs, 1992 base.*
Source: Statistics Canada, Catalogue no. 13-207-XPB.

Table 7.10

Percentage of families with low income, 1980-1997[1]

	Families with head aged 65 and over	Families with head under age 65					
		Couples without children	Couples with children	Couples with other relatives	Total couples	Lone-parent with male head	Lone-parent with female head
	%						
1980	19.2	6.7	9.7	4.1	12.4	25.4	57.3
1981	20.4	7.3	10.2	4.2	12.1	18.7	53.5
1982	14.9	8.9	11.9	4.9	14.1	26.1	59.3
1983	15.5	9.6	12.6	6.0	15.1	28.6	60.7
1984	16.9	9.9	13.1	6.1	15.6	27.0	62.3
1985	15.2	8.5	11.8	4.7	14.3	26.9	61.1
1986	14.3	9.0	10.9	4.3	13.4	23.4	57.7
1987	12.9	9.0	10.3	4.5	13.2	18.4	58.3
1988	12.8	7.9	9.1	3.1	12.1	24.3	55.3
1989	10.1	7.3	8.7	2.8	11.3	20.3	52.9
1990	7.6	8.1	9.8	3.2	13.1	25.5	59.5
1991	8.2	9.1	10.8	3.7	13.8	22.6	60.3
1992	8.7	8.6	10.6	5.6	14.4	18.9	56.9
1993	9.7	9.6	12.2	3.6	15.5	30.9	59.0
1994	7.1	9.4	11.5	5.5	14.6	32.2	56.4
1995	7.8	10.1	12.8	5.2	15.4	30.7	56.8
1996	8.7	10.0	11.8	5.3	15.5	31.3	60.8
1997	6.8	10.6	12.0	5.3	15.3	23.5	56.0

[1] *Based on Statistics Canada's Low Income Cut-offs, 1992 base.*
Source: Statistics Canada, Catalogue no. 13-207-XPB.

Table 7.11

Family expenditures, 1997

	Families with head		Unattached individuals aged		Unattached seniors	
	Under age 65	Aged 65 and over	15-64	65 and over	Men	Women
			%			
Food	11.2	13.2	10.3	14.1	12.7	14.7
Shelter	19.4	17.1	22.8	26.4	21.7	28.5
Household operation	4.6	4.4	4.1	5.6	4.5	6.1
Household furnishings and equipment	2.7	2.9	2.5	2.3	2.2	2.4
Clothing	4.5	4.1	3.7	3.6	2.2	4.3
Transportation	12.6	14.2	10.6	8.5	11.5	7.1
Health care	2.1	3.9	2.0	4.1	3.3	4.4
Personal care	1.3	1.4	1.2	1.8	0.7	2.3
Recreation	5.7	5.1	5.4	4.1	4.7	3.8
Reading material	0.5	0.7	0.7	0.9	1.0	0.9
Education	1.6	0.4	0.8	0.1	--	0.1
Tobacco products and alcoholic beverages	2.2	2.1	3.2	1.7	2.3	1.4
Game of chance (net)	0.4	0.8	0.6	0.8	0.9	0.8
Miscellaneous	1.5	1.7	1.9	1.5	1.6	1.5
Personal taxes	22.1	17.7	21.9	13.1	18.6	10.6
Security	5.9	4.3	5.3	2.7	1.1	3.4
Gifts and contributions	1.7	5.9	3.0	8.9	10.8	8.0
Total	100.0	100.0	100.0	100.0	100.0	100.0

Source: Statistics Canada, Income Statistics Division.

Senior Lifestyles

Leisure time of seniors

Seniors generally have more leisure time than people in younger age ranges. In a 1992 survey, people aged 65 and over had an average of 7.7 hours of free time per day, more than two hours more per day than the figure for those between the ages of 15 and 64[1].

Seniors watching television

Television viewing accounts for the largest share of the free time of older persons. In 1997, people aged 60 and over watched television an average of 4.9 hours per day, almost two hours more per day than the figure for those between the ages of 18 and 59. (Chart 8.1)

Women in older age ranges generally watch more television than their male counterparts. In 1997, women aged 60 and over averaged 5.2 hours per day watching television, compared with 4.6 hours for men in this age range.

News and public affairs account for the largest share of the television-viewing time of older Canadians. In 1997, 44% of the viewing time of people aged 60 and over, more than 2 hours per day, was devoted to news and public affairs. In fact, people aged 60 and over were more than twice as likely to watch this type of programming as those between the ages of 18 and 59. (Chart 8.2)

Of the remaining television-viewing time of people aged 60 and over, 20% was spent watching dramas, 10% went to each of sports and variety and game shows, 6% was devoted to comedies, and 5% went to either documentaries or instructional television. Of these types of programming, people aged 60 and over were more likely than their counterparts between the ages of 18 and 59 to watch sports and instructional shows, while they were less likely to watch all other types of programming.

Physical activity of seniors

Many seniors, however, are also physically active on a regular basis. In 1997, half (50%) of all people aged 65 and over engaged in regular physical activity, while 12% occasionally took part in such activity. (Table 8.1)

In fact, seniors are only slightly less likely than people in younger age ranges to be physically active on a regular basis. In 1997, 50% of seniors participated in these types of activities on a regular basis, compared with around 55% of those between the ages of 25 and 64 and 66% of 15- to 24-year-olds.

---

[1] *For more information on the time use patterns of seniors see "As Time Goes By: Time Use of Canadians" by Judith A. Frederick, Statistics Canada, Catalogue no. 89-544-XPE.*

Chart 8.1

Average number of hours per day spent watching television, 1997

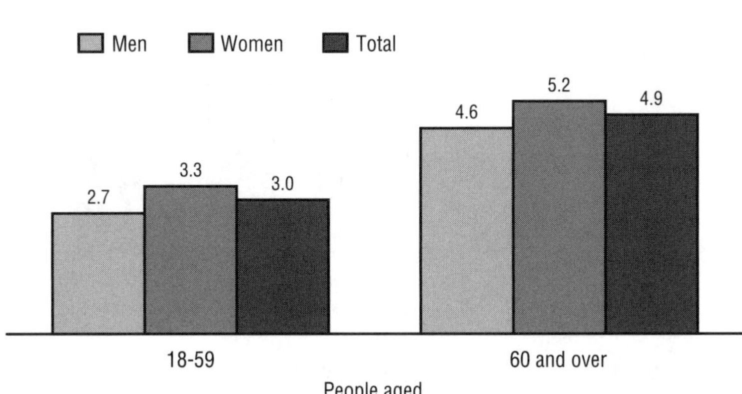

Source: Statistics Canada, Education, Culture and Tourism Division.

Chart 8.2

Distribution of television viewing time, by type of program, 1997

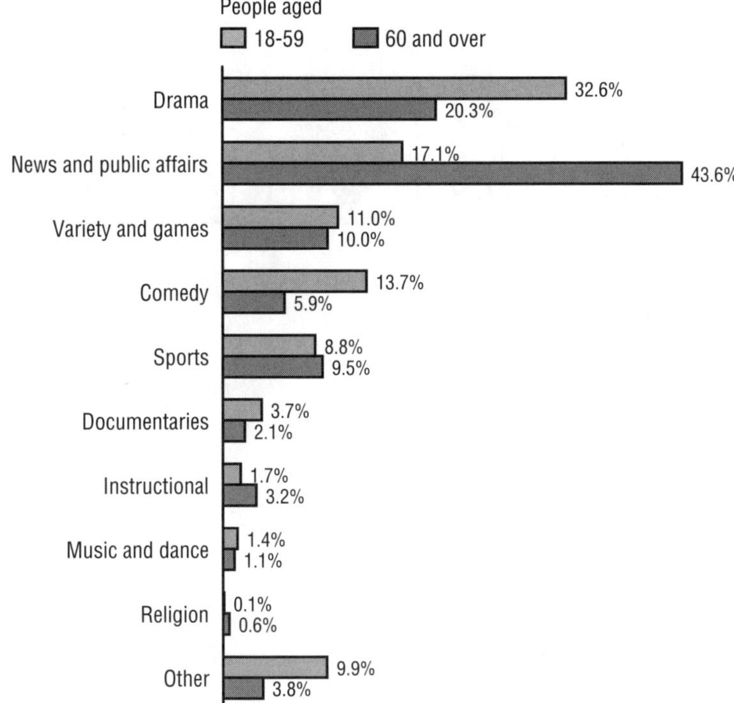

Source: Statistics Canada, Education, Culture and Tourism Division.

Among seniors, men are slightly more likely than women to undertake physical activities on a regular basis. In 1997, 53% of men aged 65 and over participated in regular physical activities, compared with 47% of senior women.

Participation in religious activities by seniors

Seniors are also very involved in religious activities. In 1996, 37% of people aged 65 and over attended church or other religious functions at least once a week. This was about the same figure as for those aged 55 to 64 (36%), but well above figures for people aged 45 to 54 (21%), 25 to 44 (16%), and 15 to 24 (12%). (Table 8.2)

Senior women are more likely than their male counterparts to attend religious activities on a regular basis. In 1996, 42% of women aged 65 and over, versus 30% of senior men, attended such functions on a weekly basis.

Seniors are also the most likely age group to make a contribution to their church or synagogue. In 1997, 40% of all seniors made a financial contribution to their church, synagogue, mosque, or other place of worship[2].

Travel of seniors

Seniors are traveling within Canada somewhat more often than they did in the past. In 1997, seniors made an average of just under 3 trips per person within Canada. This was down slightly from the early 1990s, but it was almost a full trip more per person, on average, than in the early 1980s. (Table 8.3)

Seniors, though, are still somewhat less likely than people in younger age ranges to travel domestically. In 1997, seniors made an average of 3 domestic trips, compared with around 5 trips per person among those between the ages of 25 and 64 and 4 trips per person for 15- to 24-year-olds.

On the other hand, seniors are about as likely as younger people to travel internationally. In 1997, people aged 65 and over made an average of 0.7 international trips per person, compared with around 1 trip per person, on average, among those aged 45 to 64 and 0.6 trips per person for 25- to 44-year-olds. (Chart 8.3)

---

2 *Source: Statistics Canada, 1997 National Survey on Giving, Volunteering, and Participating.*

Almost all travel undertaken by seniors is for personal reasons. In 1997, 95% of all domestic trips made by seniors in 1997 were for personal reasons. That year, 44% of these trips involved visiting friends or relatives, 34% were for pleasure, and 18% were for other personal activities. (Table 8.4)

Similarly, personal reasons accounted for 92% of all international trips made by seniors in 1997. Of these trips, 52% were for holidays or vacations, 24% were to visit family or friends, and 16% were for other personal reasons. The remaining international trips were either for business (4%) or other reasons (4%). (Table 8.5)

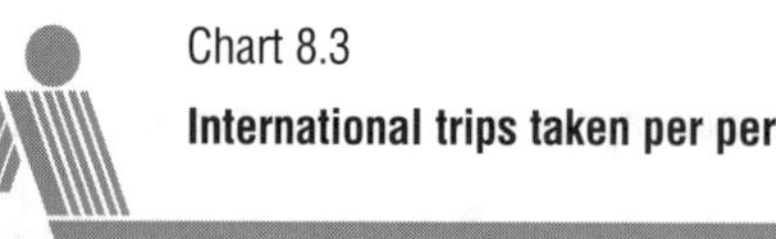

Chart 8.3

International trips taken per person, 1997

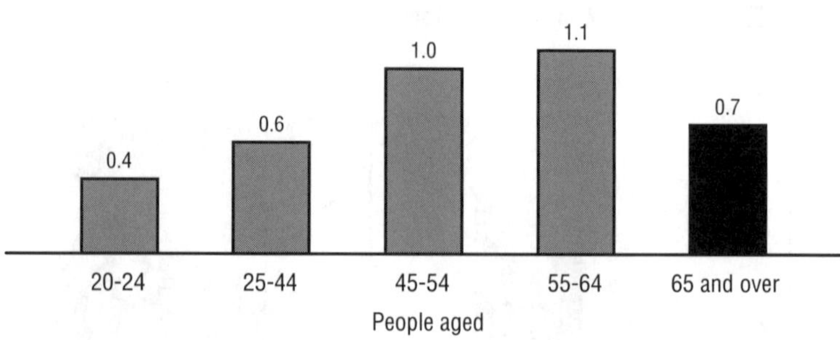

Source: Statistics Canada, Education, Culture and Tourism Division.

Criminal victimization and the fear of crime among seniors

Seniors are generally less likely than people in younger age ranges to be the victims of a crime. For example, in 1997, there were 1.5 senior homicide victims for every 100,000 people aged 65 and over, compared with 2.6 among 15- to 24-year-olds, 2.4 among those aged 25 to 44, and 1.7 among those aged 45 to 64. (Chart 8.4)

Senior men are more likely than senior women to be the victims of a homicide. In 1997, there were 2.3 murder victims for every 100,000 men aged 65 and over, compared with a figure of 0.9 among women in this age range.

Seniors are also much less likely than people in younger age ranges to be the victim of an attack on their person or property. In 1993, 6% of people aged 65 and over were victims of a personal crime, compared with 17% of people aged 45 to 64, 27% of those aged 25 to 44, and 37% of 15- to 24-year-olds. (Table 8.6)

Chart 8.4

Homicide victims per 100,000 population, 1997

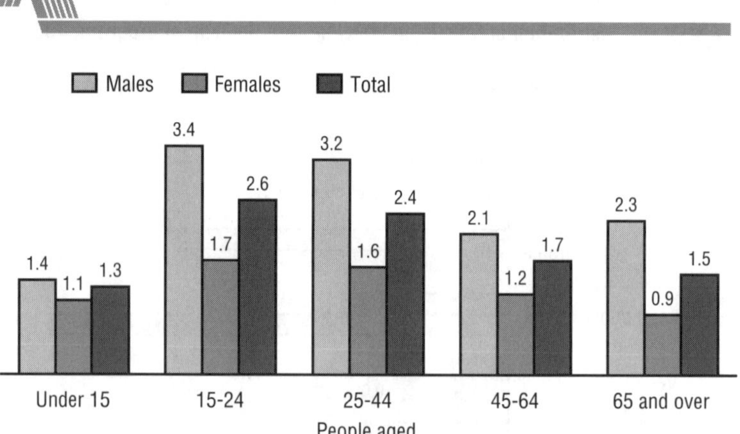

Source: Statistics Canada, Canadian Centre for Justice Statistics.

Senior men are also slightly more likely than senior women to be the victims of a personal crime. In 1993, 8% of men aged 65 and over, versus 5% of women in this age range, had been the victims of a personal crime.

While the homicide and personal victimization rates for seniors are lower than those for people in younger age ranges, seniors are more likely than younger people to feel unsafe when walking alone in their neighbourhoods after dark. In 1993, 41% of people aged 65 and over said that they felt either very or somewhat unsafe when walking alone in their neighbourhoods after dark, compared with 26% of those aged 45 to 64 and 23% of those in age groups under age 45. (Table 8.7)

Female seniors are considerably more likely than their male contemporaries to feel unsafe when walking alone in their neighbourhood after dark. In 1993, over half (57%) of women aged 65 and over, as opposed to 19% of men in this age range, reported feeling unsafe when alone on their neighbourhood streets after dark.

Fewer seniors, however, feel worried when home alone at night. In 1993, 23% of people aged 65 and over said that they were either very or somewhat worried about being home alone at night, slightly below figures reported by younger people. (Table 8.8)

Chart 8.5

Percentage of households with selected technological equipment, 1997

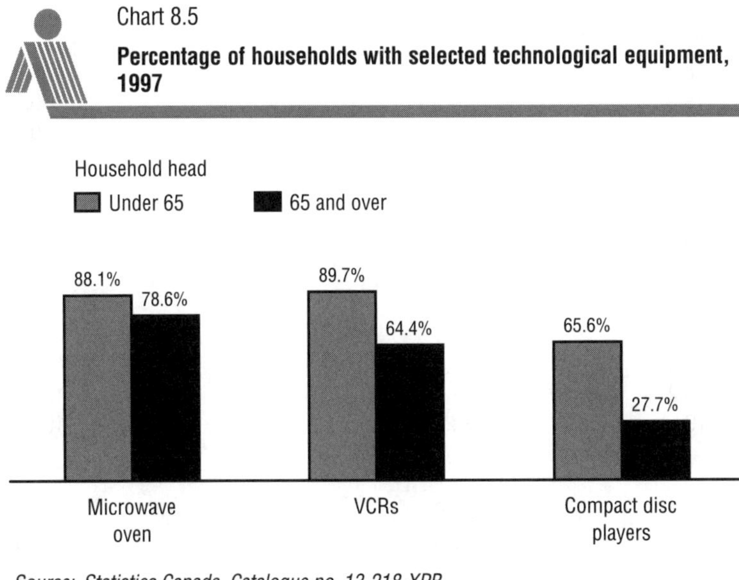

Source: Statistics Canada, Catalogue no. 13-218-XPB.

Again, senior women are more likely than senior men to feel unsafe when at home alone. In 1993, 27% of women aged 65 and over reported feeling unsafe when home alone after dark, compared with 17% of men in this age range. Senior women, though, were less likely than women in age groups under age 65 to report concerns about their safety when home alone, whereas senior men were more concerned about their safety when home alone at night than their younger counterparts.

Seniors and new technologies

Many seniors own technologically innovative equipment such as microwave ovens, VCRs, and CD players. In 1997, for example, 79% of households with head aged 65 and over had a microwave oven and 64% had a VCR. Only 28%, though, had a CD player. Senior households, however, are still less likely than younger households to have these facilities. (Chart 8.5)

Table 8.1

Percentage of people living in a private household participating in physical activities, by frequency, 1996-1997

	Frequency of physical activity				
	Regular	Occasional	Rarely	Not Stated	Total
			%		
People aged:					
15-24					
Men	67.8	16.0	12.7	3.5	100.0
Women	64.6	19.0	14.9	1.5	100.0
Total	66.2	17.4	13.8	2.5	100.0
25-44					
Men	54.1	23.1	20.6	2.2	100.0
Women	60.0	19.2	19.4	1.4	100.0
Total	57.1	21.2	20.0	1.7	100.0
45-54					
Men	50.8	20.8	24.3	4.1	100.0
Women	58.3	18.2	22.1	1.4	100.0
Total	54.5	19.6	23.3	2.7	100.0
55-64					
Men	55.9	17.1	23.6	3.3	100.0
Women	57.8	17.4	23.0	1.8	100.0
Total	56.9	17.3	23.3	2.5	100.0
65 and over					
Men	52.7	12.0	26.7	8.5	100.0
Women	47.2	12.2	35.8	4.8	100.0
Total	49.6	12.1	31.9	6.4	100.0

Source: Statistics Canada, Catalogue no. 82-221-XPE.

Table 8.2

Percentage of people attending religious activities, by frequency, 1996

	Once a week or more	Once a month	A few times/ once a year	Not at all	Other[1]	Total
			%			
People aged:						
15-24						
Men	12.1	11.4	28.3	24.2	24.1	100.0
Women	12.7	8.1	30.1	26.7	22.4	100.0
Total	12.4	9.8	29.2	25.4	23.3	100.0
25-44						
Men	13.8	9.5	28.2	29.8	18.7	100.0
Women	17.9	9.6	29.3	27.9	15.3	100.0
Total	15.8	9.6	28.7	28.8	17.0	100.0
45-54						
Men	16.8	8.1	26.7	33.2	15.1	100.0
Women	25.6	10.4	27.5	25.0	11.4	100.0
Total	21.2	9.3	27.1	29.2	13.3	100.0
55-64						
Men	27.4	12.6	24.0	26.2	9.9	100.0
Women	40.9	10.9	22.3	20.1	5.8	100.0
Total	35.7	12.1	20.7	23.7	7.9	100.0
65 and over						
Men	30.2	11.4	20.6	27.4	10.3	100.0
Women	41.5	11.4	18.6	23.6	4.9	100.0
Total	36.6	11.4	19.4	25.3	7.2	100.0

[1] *Includes those with no religious affiliation.*
Source: Statistics Canada, General Social Survey, 1996.

Table 8.3

Domestic trips taken per person, 1982-1997

	1982	1984	1986	1988	1990	1992	1994	1996	1997
	Trips per person								
People aged:									
15-24	3.7	3.2	4.3	4.4	4.1	5.3	5.1	4.4	4.0
25-44	5.1	4.7	5.4	6.0	5.7	6.8	6.1	5.4	5.0
45-54	4.5	4.5	5.3	5.9	6.3	7.2	6.4	5.8	5.2
55-64	4.1	3.7	4.6	4.9	4.6	5.4	6.0	5.1	4.8
65-69	3.3	2.9	3.7	4.1	4.1	4.8	4.4	4.1	3.8
70 and over	1.5	1.4	1.8	1.9	2.1	2.7	2.5	2.4	2.3
Total 65 and over	2.2	1.9	2.4	2.7	2.8	3.4	3.2	2.9	2.8

Sources: Statistics Canada, Catalogue nos. 87-504-XPB and 91-537-XPB; and Education, Culture and Tourism Division .

Table 8.4

Distribution of domestic trips, by reason for travel, 1997

	Reason for trip				
	Visiting friends/ relatives	Pleasure	Personal	Business/ conventions	Total
	%				
People aged:					
15-24	38.4	42.9	13.5	5.1	100.0
25-44	33.6	34.1	12.5	19.8	100.0
45-54	29.8	33.6	13.9	22.6	100.0
55-64	38.1	31.3	14.0	16.6	100.0
65-69	41.4	35.1	17.0	6.5	100.0
70 and over	45.5	32.2	18.3	3.9	100.0
Total 65 and over	43.8	33.5	17.8	5.0	100.0

Source: Statistics Canada, Education, Culture and Tourism Division.

Table 8.5

Distribution of international trips, by reason for travel, 1997

	Reason for trip					
	Visiting friends/ relatives	Holiday/ vacation	Other personal[1]	Business/ conventions	Other	Total
	%					
People aged:						
20-24	22.8	47.9	14.2	8.3	6.8	100.0
25-44	15.4	44.2	11.6	25.3	3.4	100.0
45-54	15.8	45.4	13.6	21.2	3.9	100.0
55-64	18.7	50.6	14.9	11.4	4.4	100.0
65 and over	23.7	52.2	15.7	4.1	4.4	100.0

1 *Includes visits to second homes and cottages; attending events or other attractions; education or study; medical reasons; to attend family occasions such as weddings; and shopping.*

Source: Statistics Canada, Education, Culture and Tourism Division.

Table 8.6

Percentage of people who were victims of personal crimes, 1993

	Once	Two or more times	Total
		%	
People aged:			
15-24			
Men	23	14	38
Women	21	16	37
Total	22	15	37
25-44			
Men	19	7	27
Women	19	9	28
Total	19	8	27
45-64			
Men	14	5	19
Women	12	4	16
Total	13	5	17
65 and over			
Men	6	--	8
Women	4	--	5
Total	5	--	6

Source: Statistics Canada, General Social Survey, 1993.

Table 8.7

Percentage of people who felt safe/unsafe when walking alone in their neighbourhood after dark, 1993

	Proportion feeling					
	Very unsafe	Somewhat unsafe	Reasonably safe	Very safe	Don't know/ not stated	Total
			%			
People aged:						
15-24						
Men	--	5	43	50	--	100
Women	14	26	45	14	--	100
Total	8	15	44	33	--	100
25-44						
Men	3	6	40	51	--	100
Women	14	25	44	17	1	100
Total	8	15	42	34	1	100
45-64						
Men	4	7	42	47	--	100
Women	20	21	40	17	2	100
Total	12	14	41	32	1	100
65 and over						
Men	10	9	37	38	6	100
Women	38	19	22	13	7	100
Total	26	15	29	24	7	100

Source: Statistics Canada, General Social Survey, 1993.

Table 8.8

Percentage of people who worried/didn't worry when home alone at night, 1993

	Proportion feeling		
	Very or somewhat worried	Not at all worried	Total
		%	
People aged:			
15-24			
Men	11	89	100
Women	42	58	100
Total	27	74	100
25-44			
Men	11	89	100
Women	39	61	100
Total	25	75	100
45-64			
Men	11	89	100
Women	37	63	100
Total	24	76	100
65 and over			
Men	17	83	100
Women	27	73	100
Total	23	77	100

Source: Statistics Canada, General Social Survey, 1993.

ORDER FORM

Statistics Canada

TO ORDER:

MAIL

Statistics Canada
Operations and Integration
Circulation Management
120 Parkdale Avenue
Ottawa, Ontario
Canada K1A 0T6

PHONE
1 800 267-6677

Charge to VISA or MasterCard. Outside Canada and the U.S., and in the Ottawa area, call (613) 951-7277. Please do not send confirmation.

FAX
1 800 889-9734

or (613) 951-1584. VISA, MasterCard and purchase orders only. Please do not send confirmation. A fax will be treated as an original order.

INTERNET order@statcan.ca

1 800 363-7629
Telecommunication Device for the Hearing Impaired

(Please print)

Company ______________________

Department ______________________

Attention ______________ Title ______________

Address ______________________

City ______________ Province ______________

Postal Code ________ Phone ( ) ________ Fax ( ) ________

E-mail address: ______________________

METHOD OF PAYMENT:

(Check only one)

☐ **Please charge my:** ☐ VISA ☐ MasterCard

Card Number ______________________

Expiry Date ______________________

Cardholder *(please print)* ______________________

Signature ______________________

☐ **Payment enclosed $** ______________________

☐ **Purchase Order Number** ______________________
(please enclose)

Authorized Signature ______________________

Catalogue Number	Title	Date of issue or indicate an "S" for subscription	Price (All prices exclude sales tax)		Quantity	Total $
			Canada $	Outside Canada US$		

Note: Catalogue prices for clients outside Canada are shown in US dollars. Clients outside Canada pay total amount in US funds drawn on a US bank.	SUBTOTAL	
Subscription will begin with the next issue to be released.	DISCOUNT (if applicable)	
Prices are subject to change. To Confirm current prices call 1 800 267-6677.	GST (7%) (Canadian clients only, where applicable)	
Canadian clients pay in Canadian funds and add 7% GST and applicable PST or HST.	Applicable PST (Canadian clients only, where applicable)	
	Applicable HST (N.S., N.B., Nfld.)	
Cheque or money order should be made payable to the *Receiver General for Canada.*	GRAND TOTAL	
GST Registration # R121491807	PF 097177	

THANK YOU FOR YOUR ORDER!

Statistics Canada Statistique Canada

BON DE COMMANDE

Statistique Canada

POUR COMMANDER :

COURRIER

Statistique Canada
Opérations et intégration
Gestion de la circulation
120, avenue Parkdale
Ottawa (Ontario)
Canada K1A 0T6

TÉLÉPHONE
1 800 267-6677

Faites débiter votre compte VISA ou MasterCard. De l'extérieur du Canada et des États-Unis et dans la région d'Ottawa, composez le (613) 951-7277. Veuillez ne pas envoyer de confirmation.

TÉLÉCOPIEUR
1 800 889-9734

ou (613) 951-1584. VISA, MasterCard et bon de commande seulement. Veuillez ne pas envoyer de confirmation. Le bon télécopié tient lieu de commande originale.

INTE

(Veuillez éc

Compa

Servic

À l'atte

Adress

Ville

Code p

Adresse

70847

MODALITÉS DE PAIEMENT :

(Cochez une seule case)

☐ **Veuillez débiter mon compte** ☐ VISA ☐ MasterCard

N° de carte

Date d'expiration

Détenteur de carte *(en majuscules s.v.p.)*

Signature

☐ **Paiement inclus $** ____________

☐ **N° du bon de commande** ____________
(veuillez joindre le bon)

Signature de la personne autorisée

Numéro catalog		Prix (Les prix n'incluent pas la taxe de vente)		Quantité	Total $
	s s	Canada $	Extérieur du Canada $ US		

▶ Veuillez noter que les prix au catalogue pour les clients de l'extérieur du Canada sont donnés en dollars américains. Les clients de l'extérieur du Canada paient le montant total en dollars US tirés sur une banque américaine.	TOTAL	
▶ L'abonnement commencera avec le prochain numéro diffusé.	RÉDUCTION (s'il y a lieu)	
▶ Les prix peuvent être modifiés sans préavis. Pour vérifier les prix courants, veuillez composer le 1 800 267-6677.	TPS (7 %) (Clients canadiens seulement, s'il y a lieu)	
▶ Les clients canadiens paient en dollars canadiens et ajoutent soit la TPS de 7 % et la TVP en vigueur, soit la TVH.	TVP en vigueur (Clients canadiens seulement, s'il y a lieu)	
	TVH en vigueur (N.-É., N.-B., T.-N.)	
▶ Le chèque ou mandat-poste doit être établi à l'ordre du *Receveur général du Canada.*	TOTAL GÉNÉRAL	
▶ TPS N° R121491807	**PF097177**	

MERCI DE VOTRE COMMANDE!

Statistique Canada Statistics Canada

Canada